"DESIGN YOUR FUTURE is an insightful—and yet easily read and fun—book which step by step takes you through the art of creating your life. Read it and you'll have a most enjoyable learning experience!"

-Rolf Österberg
Author, *Corporate Renaissance:*
Business as an Adventure in Human Development
President & CEO, Svensk Filmindustri

"DESIGN YOUR FUTURE is an excellent introduction to the role of vision and the power of thought in realizing our unique potential as individuals.

. . . .

"It offers a valuable alternative vision that helps to move us away from the competitive orientation of contemporary society.

. . . .

"Siegel is that rarest of rare creatures: a realistic visionary, able to translate his vision into very practical guidelines and suggestions.

. . . .

"He writes in a compelling, imaginative, readable, and non-sexist prose.

. . . .

"He has a firm grounding in the new paradigm, with its premium on inner authority, cooperation, community, ethical sensitivity and globalism.

. . . .

"DESIGN YOUR FUTURE is a clarion call for change, painting an indelible picture of the emerging LEARNING SOCIETY for which we all should be preparing."

-Sue Mehrtens
Co-Author, *The Fourth Wave*
President, The Potlatch Group

"DESIGN YOUR FUTURE more than lives up to its name. It is a mind-stretching landmark book.

. . . .

"Beware! This book is not for the fainthearted. It can lead you and equip you for **greatness!**..It leads the reader all the way from self-discovery to self-fulfillment and, ultimately, to self-actualization.

. . . .

"Siegel clearly sees what the rest of us must learn to see. That is, the future is all about the *mind* and it's nurturing and development.

. . . .

"Here is a rich smorgasbord of mental, emotional, and spiritual nourishment - a treasure trove of challenges, insights, and tools for the optimization of the self."

-Joe Batten
Author, *Tough Minded Leadership*

DESIGN YOUR FUTURE

LIVE YOUR *VISION*

in the ever-changing *LEARNING SOCIETY*

by

PAUL "THE SOARING" SIEGEL

DESIGN YOUR FUTURE
Live Your Vision
in the ever-changing *LEARNING SOCIETY*
by PAUL "THE SOARING" SIEGEL

© Copyright 1994 by Paul Siegel

Available from your bookstore or direct from the publisher:

Learning Society Publications
3461 Marna Avenue, Suite 102
Long Beach, CA 90808

Library of Congress Cataloging-in-Publication Data

Siegel, Paul
Design your future
Live your vision in the ever-changing learning society
Includes index
1. Business.   2. Personal improvement.   3. Success
650.1'3   HF5386
Library of Congress Catalog Card No. 94-76685

ISBN# 0-9623769-6-5

Printed in USA
Price: $17.95

To Evelyn
my wife and companion
...................*for soaring*

and to all others
seeking wings
...................*for soaring*

ACKNOWLEDGEMENTS

I want to acknowledge the help I received from many people. During the book's first stages, I was supported by the helpful evaluations and suggestions of entrepreneur Kathy Blank and many professional speakers, among whom are Burt Dubin, Allen Willey, Lynn Banker, Ted Kagan, and Gary Lockwood. Later, the book was reviewed by Bernard Raskin, John Rennebu, Ev Morris, and Roy King of the National Writers Association. I also received lots of help and support from that organization's executive director, Sandy Whelchel.

I want to give special thanks to Joe Barton, Rolf Österberg, and Susan Mehrtens for their endorsements and strong support. Finally, I want to thank my wife, Evelyn, without whose endurance this book could not have been published.

FOREWORD

The future can be a daunting and fearsome place if we stay crouched down behind obsolete paradigms and stereotypes.

Conversely, and happily, the future can be rich in opportunities, discoveries, fulfillment and joy. There are currently tens of millions searching, all too often futilely, for a better way.

This book by Paul Siegel is rich in insights, growth factors, and tools to provide just what these millions of people are aching for. It is a book about vision, values, vitality, and voltage. He offers a complete smorgasbord of tools for the mind, heart, and spirit.

His treatment of topics like vision, learning, and leadership is not a stale re-hash served up from the past. Rather, he invites readers to let their minds soar into the year 2020.

In all of my 36 years as a consultant, trainer, author, and speaker throughout the world, I have had many opportunities to meet and mentor a wide assortment of leaders.

Design Your Future will be high on the list of books I will recommend to leaders who aspire to greatness and to all those who simply want a better future.

You are urged to read it again and again.

-Joe Batten
Author, *Tough-Minded Leadership*

TABLE OF CONTENTS

Chapter 1

Design For *Success*

Bill Clinton is president of the United States. Is he a success?

Meryl Streep won an Academy Award as Best Actress. Is she a success?

Ross Perot has billions of dollars. Is he a success?

Steve Jobs, is the boy-wonder entrepreneur who, together with Steve Wozniak, founded Apple Computer Company. Is he a success?

YOU—are you a success?

I believe that you can answer only the last question; none of the others. Success is not an objective thing. It is subjective and within grasp of every person. The thesis of this book is that you can design your success: the type of future you have been dreaming about. Furthermore, high technology is so transforming our society that now you can dream bigger more fanciful dreams! The more wonderful your dreams, the more brilliant your success.

ONLY YOU CAN DEFINE *SUCCESS*

The vast majority of books about success push you to be as competitive as possible. They push you to beat your opponents, reach the top, become the best, number one. They push you to be an entrepreneur, a winner. They push you to seek power, fame, money and achievement.

None of these things defines success. ou are not a success if you win according to criteria promulgated by others. Becoming the best at some activity does not make you a success. Life is not a contest between you and everyone else. If you win, make money, or become famous, you are not necessarily a success. Trying to be number one will drive you frantic with frustration. It will not make you a success.

Christopher Morley said it wisely:

> There is only one success—to be able to spend your
> life in your own way.

The way YOU want it. Not other people. Forget about what other people think. What they think is unimportant. Only what YOU think counts.

Success is a matter of excellence. But the whole subject of excellence has been distorted. Excellence is not knowing how to compete, how to become a champion, how to set goals, how to spend a lifetime striving to reach ever bigger goals. Big TO-DO lists do not encourage excellence. If you think in terms of goals you limit yourself. Do what you enjoy and what excites you and you will do it excellently.

Excellence is

* not being better than anyone else, but being the best YOU can be

* not being good at what others decide is important, but at what YOU consider important

* not besting anyone else, but doing what YOU enjoy.

Success is not an achievement, but a way of life. Not an objective thing, but a subjective idea. Not a result, but a process.

Success is living your personal vision!

PAINT A VISION

What is a vision? A vision is your purpose for living. A vision is what you want to be and do. It gives zest and meaning to each day. It springs you out of bed each morning eager to go. A vision guides you through your life. It is a script of your life's drama. A way of life.

A vision is a dream. We all have dreams. We dream at night. We dream in the daytime. We dream of all the wonderful things we will accomplish or that will happen to us. Dreams give us a chance to shake off our routine activities. Dreams enable us to stretch our imaginations. They enable us to forget our troubles and heartbreaks. They enable us to boast, puff out our chests and feel good about ourselves.

And then they fade away. If they do, obviously these dreams are not visions. To become a vision, a dream must excite you to action. If you have a dream—and who doesn't?—regardless of how extravagant and far-fetched it may appear to be, you can convert it into a vision. As the famous Napoleon Hill said:

> Whatever the mind of man can conceive and believe,
> he can achieve.

It is entirely up to you. Paint a vision of what you most desire. Don't look at where you are now, the so-called reality. Visualize the future through your mind and your eyes. Your aspirations can be as high as you want them to be. The vision you paint can be your reality. You can make it grand. You can achieve it. You can design your future.

DESIGN—DON'T PLAN

Designing is different from planning. When you plan, you start by defining where you are and make changes to bring yourself closer to what you forecast for the future. When you design, you start by defining what you want your future to be and then proceed to work your way towards it. When you plan, you adapt yourself to uncertain external forces. When you design, you adapt known external forces to what you desire. When you plan, you are trying to achieve set goals. When you design, you are looking for yourself to live according to your vision of the future.

You don't need to plan for an uncertain future.

You can DESIGN it as you desire it!

I am often asked in my workshops on future design to list the major steps to follow. There aren't any. There are no cookbooks, six steps or ten steps to follow to design your future. Nobody knows as well as YOU what you desire and how to get it. This book explains the elements of future design and offers suggestions for designing your future around a vision. It includes ways

444

in which you may use high technology to magnify your vision. Choose your own vision and in your own way make it grand.

TECHNOLOGY IS AT YOUR SERVICE

Technology will definitely affect your vision.

The media bombards us with bugaboos about technology. The problems presented by the detractors are not as bad as they have made them out to be. Let's look at three big bugaboos:

Bugaboo #1: Change Induces Stress

Change, change, change.

Change is what everyone is talking about. Change is what everyone is writing about. Change is what we hear about on radio and on TV. Change is what we see in the garage, the shopping center, the supermarket, the roads, the airways, the kitchen, the newspaper. We are being smothered with messages about change in technology, in organizations, in our working conditions, in our leisure activities, in our life styles, in our values, in our lives.

We hear it said that what we know becomes obsolete after eighteen months. We hear that this constant change keeps hitting us at an ever increasing rate. At one time we were told that we needed to change careers every five years. The new message is that we must change careers every three years. What does this portend for the future? Knowledge will eventually be good for a month and a career change will be good for a season?

From all we hear, change is bad for us. It makes our jobs obsolete, fractures families, disturbs our relationships with other people, increases stress, ruins our health. The recommended solution is to slow down: find a way to avoid, at least for some period, the many changes taking place. Robert Fulghum, in his best seller, *All I Need to Know I Learned in Kindergarten*, tells you to go back to the simple life. In other words, he advises you to withdraw from society for the sake of your health.

But who wants to go back to the horse-and-buggy days? There is a better way to handle change: learn about it. The best protection against change is not to escape to some quiet place or drop out of active involvement, but to arm yourself with understanding. Lack of understanding of what is happening is the main

reason for stress. Once you do understand, you can come up
with answers to questions like these:

* How did it happen?

* What is the principle behind the new idea?

* Is this just a new version of the same old gadget?

* What are the drawbacks to its use?

* How is it related to other forces in our society?

* How will it affect my future?

If you can answer such questions your dread of change fades,
disappears and is obliterated. You begin to see that much of what
is called change is merely cosmetic, repetitious, or of little
consequence. You begin to see that real change is healthy, good
and a positive source of joy.

Bugaboo #2: Robots Replace Blue-Collars

Robots, robots, robots.

Robots are getting smarter. Robots are getting more skillful.
Robots are doing more in the factory. Robots are replacing
people. Complete factories are being built where all the production is done by robots, with only a handful of people.

Robots indeed are shrinking employment in the manufacturing sector. When modern automated factories rise, the need for
the type of labor that feeds or tends the machine disappears. In
its place, rises the need for people with the knowledge to work
with these systems.

The problem is not one of robots replacing people, but of
people who don't know how to use their minds. They can't do
it because they never exercise their minds. For those who are
ready to learn how to be better thinkers, problem solvers and
innovative creators, the possibilities are endless.

And you don't have to be a genius to be able to take advantage
of these opportunities. You need only reorient your thinking.

Bugaboo #3: AI Replaces White Collars

AI, AI, AI.

AI is the affectionate term used for artificial intelligence. With AI we are able to get machines to think. AI can solve problems for us. AI gives us intellectual control over machines. AI makes possible machines that can learn. With AI we can build robots that behave like humans—intelligent robots.

Now that we have intelligent robots, some people say, who needs the intelligence of people? But they are wrong. If robots become smarter, it will be because people will design intelligence into them. As robots become smarter, instead of replacing people they will be used by people to help them think at a higher level.

NEW OPPORTUNITIES IN THE LEARNING SOCIETY

Technology always seems to be discussed in terms of whether it is bad or good. This is too simplistic, because there has recently been a radical change in the nature of technology. Whereas before technology dealt primarily with the world of things, it is now concentrating on the world of ideas.

In previous ages, most people worked with their hands. They learned certain skills and crafts. They were nimble with their fingers, fast with their feet and strong with their muscles. Their technology amplified these physical capabilities.

In today's society we emphasize the mind. Today's technology enhances our mental capabilities.

Some say we live in the Information Society. But I disagree. It's not information that we seek, but knowledge. I do not like to call it the Knowledge Society either, since this implies that there is an objective thing out there called knowledge. This is not so. Knowledge is the product of the mind, the result of learning. I call the new society THE LEARNING SOCIETY.

In THE LEARNING SOCIETY there will be many new opportunities for intellectual achievement. Here are but glimpses of possibilities:

ARTIST—The computer promises to become the ultimate artistic medium, available to almost everyone.

BANKER—Global information networks will make money a matter of information and reduce paper work.

ENTREPRENEUR—Instead of building big organizations, entrepreneurs will develop flexible networks for solving urgent problems.

ENGINEER—She will enter a concept into a machine, which in one step, will produce a finished product.

HANDICAPPED—An intelligent robot will help a blind person in household tasks, reading, running the computer, and in guiding him across streets better than any seeing-eye dog.

PHYSICIAN—She may be a wellness consultant, advising clients about what they can do to preserve their own health.

PROFESSOR—He may be a learning consultant, advising clients about learning programs to follow in order to realize their visions.

SALESMAN—She will be a problem solver, tackling an urgent problem of the prospect.

WRITER—Information will be distributed primarily electronically, thus allowing the tailoring of "books".

THE FOUR ELEMENTS OF FUTURE DESIGN

It's a new world of technology. Technology is bound to affect your vision. But the nature of your vision is entirely yours. And the clearer the picture you paint of your vision the easier it will be for you to design your future. Vision is the first and most important of four elements. It is the element around which the other three elements revolve.

But having a vision alone is not enough. You need a means for achieving your vision. The way to do this is to embark upon a lifetime of learning. You need to learn about yourself, your environment and everything related to your vision.

To help us learn, we have depended on learning tools such as books. But now we have the most powerful learning system ever invented: the computer. An inifinite variety of software is available to be used as learning tools. Learning tools are the third element of future design.

The last element is leadership, the ability to get other people to help you in what you want to do. Very few people in earlier times were concerned with leadership. But today it is important for each of us, regardless of what our vision is like.

Today's corporation is structured differently from yesterday's corporation. Early corporations were rigid hierarchies with a big chief on top and lots of little peons on bottom. The quality movement, the human development movement, and especially the powerful computer have diminished the hierarchy.

Therefore, it is becoming more beneficial to think of yourself, not as a member of an organization, but as a node linked to other members in the organization as well as to people outside the organization. In other words, you are part of a network. To get other people in your network to help you, you need to exercise leadership.

To summarize, the four elements of future design are:

- **VISION—to guide your future**

- **LEARNING—to achieve your vision**

- **LEARNING TOOLS—to enhance your learning**

- **LEADERSHIP—to enlist others in your vision and learning.**

Each element, together with the associated LEARNING-SOCIETY forces, is discussed in a separate section of the book.

SECTION I

VISION

To Guide Your Future

Chapter 2
A Personal Vision

What's your attitude toward life? Do you believe in luck? Do you believe that to some people good things happen such as winning the lottery, and to others only bad things happen such as getting divorced, losing a job, and being poor? Or do you believe that what happens to you in the future depends upon what you did in the past?

If you believe in luck, you need not continue reading this book. If you believe that effort is rewarded and are seeking ways to improve your effort, this book is for you. You are ready for my message if you agree with Denis Waitley who says you should say to yourself:

> Instead of just letting life happen, I'm going to *make* it happen for me.

What you want to make happen is your vision. That all encompassing description of what you think important is your vision. The things that make you happy are in your vision. Technology is placing more and more things within your reach. This means you may have a grander vision than ever before—a vision like that of

MOSES

Moses took a walk one day and saw the burning bush. He looked at it. He stared at it. He was transfixed by the burning bush and had a vision: He, Moses, would free his people from Pharoh's yoke, teach them the ways and beauties of freedom, and mold his people into a great nation.

From then on everything Moses did until the end of his life was governed by his vision. Some people say that Moses never got to see the promised land. That's not true: he saw the promised land every day he visualized his vision.

Think of Moses as he is hypnotized by the burning bush, by his vision to free his people and make them a great nation. There is fire both inside and outside Moses. The bush is burning and as Moses stares at it his insides begin to burn; he is developing a burning desire to follow his vision.

Vision is a mission on fire!

Gazing at the burning bush, Moses dreams of what life would be like with his people free and living in their new home. This stiffens his resolve and adds fuel to his vision. As he focuses intently on the burning bush it becomes to him a star to light the way and show him what he must do. It makes his vision burn strong and steady.

Moses can not take his eyes off the burning bush. It pulls him like a magnet, a magnet that produces a current which runs through his entire body to maintain the heat of his vision.

You have a vision

* when you have a burning desire to follow your DREAM

* when this dream becomes a STAR to shine the path for you to follow

* when this star is powerful enough to act as a MAGNET to keep you on course!

In previous societies, having a vision to guide your life was the privilege of a powerful few—like Moses. Since Moses had the power and the technology—two tablets—to follow through, it made sense for him to have a vision. But not for the average person. Today, technology has placed the power which comes from knowledge within the grasp of everybody. YOU may use this knowledge power to support your personal vision.

The development of vision from the days of the Industrial Revolution to now is depicted as follows:

• **The Capitalist Vision**

• **The Personal Vision**

- **YOUR Grand Vision**

THE CAPITALIST VISION

Early man began the history of technology when he picked up a log and bashed it in the head of the tiger that was pursuing him. But the great turning point in the development of technology was the discovery of fire. Fire provided the first source of power external to man. It enabled him to work with metal, wood and other materials to fashion clothing, shelter and utensils for adornment, eating, farming, and hunting.

Technological progress was slow until the Industrial Revolution, when the power of steam, electricity, chemical reaction and nuclear explosions was directed toward the development of transportation, production and communication systems. There was a surge in the production and distribution of all sorts of products, from aspirin to zippers.

The most desireable product by far was the automobile. The car became the symbol of the Industrial Society. Henry Ford is the capitalist who probably did more than anyone else to make a car cheap enough to be bought by the masses. Ford had a vision of a car in every garage. To achieve his vision, he made two unusual moves: He offered his workers five dollars for an eight-hour day, a rate higher than anyone else was paying at that time. The other move was to design a mass-production system by adapting the conveyor belt and the assembly line to car manufacturing.

As a man who owned a factory, Ford could have a capitalist vision. His vision was broad and encompassed millions of people. But the workers in his company did not have a picnic. They lived under the brutal scrutiny of a goon called Harry Bennett. Bennett tyrannized the workers with spies and an army of thugs, gangsters, and ex-convicts. Unlike Henry Ford, the boss, Ford workers never dreamed of a vision. They felt lucky if they stayed out of trouble, kept their jobs, and lived through the violent strikes.

THE PERSONAL VISION

People describe our current era as the Information Society because of what they perceive to be the main virtue of the computer: the manipulation of information. But this view is too narrow. The computer aids people in their learning. We are in THE LEARNING SOCIETY.

ENIAC, the first working computer, was developed at the University of Pennsylvania. The first commercial computer was the UNIVAC, built in the early 1950's by Eckert-Mauchly Company, a company I was privileged to work for. Between the 1950's and the 1990's, the computer became smaller, cheaper and accessible to all.

It's true that the computer ushered in many types of information systems. Companies used computers to organize information for better decision making. In addition, the computer was used as a tool for improving telephone, radio, television, satellite, and other information-communication technologies.

It's also true that the resultant free flow of information transformed our corporations and society as a whole. But the transcendent change has not been due to the computer's release of information, but its use as a vessel for an infinite number of learning tools. These learning tools place power in the individual who does the learning.

Power is being transferred from the organization to the individual!

This is the age of the individual. This is why you have the great opportunity of thinking, not merely in terms of a job or a career, but a personal vision.

Here is an example of a personal vision. The vision is that of my favorite person: Albert Einstein. I don't think Einstein ever wrote down a vision. But the following statement made by him, seems to me to express his vision:

> I can't believe God would choose to play dice with
> the world.

His vision of an orderly world is what drove him to search for fundamental principles of the universe, to show that matter and energy are different forms of the same thing, to develop the Theory of Relativity, and later to search for a broader theory which would encompass all the major forces of nature. Breathtaking!

He was a theoretical physicist who always did his "own thing", which of course was physics.

In addition to being serious about his work, he was always true to himself. Here is but one of many examples. When he visited the United States, his fame was so great, he was besieged by movie producers to be in movies. One of them offered an astronomical amount of money to get Einstein to merely stand in front of a blackboard with a piece of chalk in his hand. Einstein refused saying:

> I refuse to behave like a performing monkey.

Despite his fame as a physicist, being a family man and a humanitarian was part of Einstein's vision. Albert Einstein often had conversations with people for hours on end, not only about science, but philosophy. At one of these conversations, a fellow violinist asked Einstein:

> For what do we exist?

> > Our fellow man. Ties of sympathy link us to the destiny of others.

Einstein originally was a pacifist. But when he found out that Hitler was about to have an atomic bomb, he knew that pacifism would not work, and he modified his vision. He reluctantly advised President Roosevelt about the atomic bomb.

He enjoyed his work, as you may gather from this remark he made to some students:

> That which is acquired through pure joy of learning is generally a useful instrument in the hands of a wide-awake person.

But today you don't have to be a genius, or even a brilliant person, to have a personal vision. You can even be a policeman. Can you find anyone more mundane than a policeman? And yet here is the story of a policeman with vision who does wonders. Officer Wayne Barton, of the Pearl City section of Boca Raton, Florida, is a policeman who arrests drug dealers. Nothing unusual about this. It is his job. But is it his "job" to run an after-school program to take kids off the street? Is it his "job" to set up training programs for adults to receive high-school equivalency certificates? Is it his "job" to get the Post Office to come into Pearl City to interview potential employees? Is it his "job" to prune trees whose shade had sheltered drug dealers, and to trim back hedges behind which young people had smoked crack? Is it his "job" to read books to the local children? No, none of these things is part of his "job". But he does them.

Obviously Officer Wayne Barton doesn't think of what he's doing as a "job" but as something that conforms to his vision of making Pearl City a pleasant community with happy residents. Drug dealing and other crimes have been reduced tremendously. People feel safer and enjoy life more. And Wayne Barton has received *Parade*'s 1988 Police-Officer-of-the-Year Award and the 1990 Jefferson Award for outstanding public service.

YOUR GRAND VISION

We have come a long way from the days when only a capitalist may have a vision. Today any person can have one.

Dear reader: Do you have a personal vision? If you do, try to magnify, stretch and elaborate it. If you don't have a vision, take some time now to paint one, before continuing with this book.

Think of what you truly like to do, what you truly would like to become, how you would truly like to affect others. Then describe, paint, build, construct, develop and visualize the future you foresee for yourself.

Make it a grand vision, like that of Moses. Don't stifle it by limiting yourself to what you have been accustomed to calling a career. Don't worry about mental constraints; they will not stop you. Visualize doing your "own thing". Include other people in your vision, again like Moses.

It's amazing how many of my seminar attendees tell me goals when I ask about their visions. A goal is a specific result or event - a snapshot. A vision doesn't concern itself with outcomes, but with a way of life. It is a dramatic script.

The following principles for a grand personal vision are discussed in the next four chapters:

- **Envision Your "Own Thing"**
- **Forget Mental Constraints**
- **Affirm Your Values**
- **Make It a Movie - Not Snapshots**

After you define your vision you will be ready to learn more about how to design your future. What you read in succeeding pages will

* influence your vision

* enhance your vision

* embellish your vision.

I can safely say that your vision upon completion of this book will be grander than your vision when you started.

Chapter 3

Envision Your "Own Thing"

In this chapter I present the first principle to follow in painting your personal vision: Make your vision YOURS. Nobody else's. Moses' vision is what HE wanted to do Though he believed he was instructed, he chose to follow the instructions. Wayne Barton's vision is what HE wanted to do. He decided himself that he could make a difference in Pearl City. Einstein's vision is what HE wanted to do. He followed his imagination, which led him to new vistas.

You can follow your innermost desires. You are blessed with interminable opportunities in THE LEARNING SOCIETY. A few rules which may be helpful to you in envisioning your "own thing" are:

- **Don't Follow Others**
- **Don't Rely on Experts**
- **Don't Rely on Tests**
- **Listen to Your "Inner Voice"**

DON'T FOLLOW OTHERS

It's admirable and useful to be inspired by parents, friends and colleagues who, in your eyes, have achieved greatness. It's tempting to follow closely in their footsteps. This is a mistake. Use them as role models. A role model is a compass to point you in the proper direction. It is not a manual of instructions to follow blindly.

Parents Are Not Always Right

Often a person chooses a vision to please his father or mother. We've all seen this happen, and the results are usually disastrous. I remember a young fellow in grammar school; I will call him Max. What do children at that time know about work? And yet, every time some kid would say he wanted to be a fireman or a movie star when he grew up, Max would say he was going to be a doctor who healed the sick because his parents are saving money for that very purpose. Max never said he liked medicine and curing sick people. But I did notice he drew pictures and cartoons every chance he got. As a "dutiful" son Max later entered medical school. When he graduated medical school, his father was able to introduce him as "my son, the doctor."

Max established a practice. But he hated it. He pursued medicine for about ten years and then in desperation threw it aside and became an illustrator for a health magazine. Luckily he was able to use some of the medicine he had learned in his new vocation.

When defining your vision, don't try to please anyone but yourself. Your parents mean well. But they make mistakes like everyone else.

Role Models Are for Inspiration

This doesn't mean you shouldn't use your parents as role models. Of course you should—if you want to follow in their footsteps. Similarly you may use friends, classmates, and colleagues as role models—if you want to emulate them. Or you may read about the lives of famous people to discover more about how they lived—if you want to be inspired by them.

Remember though, that role models are not for copying, but for inspiration. Here are a handful of the world's great role models and inspiring statements expressing their visions:

MAHATMA GANDHI—"India must conquer her so-called conquerors by love. For us patriotism is the same as the love of humanity."

THOMAS JEFFERSON—"We hold these truths to be sacred and undeniable: that all men are created equal and independent, that from equal creation they derive rights inherent and inalienable, among which are the preservation of life, and liberty, and the pursuit of happiness (from the original draft of the Declaration of Independence).

SUSAN B. ANTHONY—"Men, their rights and nothing more; women, their rights and nothing less."

MARTIN LUTHER KING, JR—"I have a dream.
One day, right here in Alabama, little black boys and black girls will be able to join hands with little white boys and white girls as sisters and brothers.
I have a dream."

Copycats Lack Initiative

Again, role models are for inspiration, not for copying. You are trying to paint a vision to guide your life. Don't let your fascination with anyone cloud your judgement when thinking about what you want. As much as you may be impressed with another person, you are a different person. You are unique, with your own set of attitudes, longings, and abilities. You don't want to be a copycat.

Copycats are dependent people. They depend upon the resources of originals. Copycats almost never do as well as originals. An original generates enthusiasm; a copy generates indifference. An original—not a copy—is what you want for your vision.

Don't make comparisons, either. As Wayne A. Dyer says:

In a world of individuals, comparison makes no sense at all.

Your vision is yours alone, unique to you. After all, your vision is a representation of your life. It *is* your life. You don't want your life to be a copy of anybody.

Find the best way to express your "own thing". Even if you are not sure—and who among us *is* sure?—express it now. You will have the rest of your life to enhance your vision by learning.

DON'T RELY ON EXPERTS

In this highly technological age, it's impossible for you to learn everything you need to know in order to paint the best possible vision. You need to be guided by experts in many different fields.

But what experts do best is discover principles and classify. Human-behavior experts have their little tests whereby they divide people and put them into slots according to their pet theories about human behavior: attitude, mental capacity, thinking capabilities, behavioral patterns, approaches to decision-making, human responsiveness, creativity - - - - - - - - - - - - the list drones on. Here are a few of the more popular pigeon holes:

Mental	Emotional
Thinking	Acting
Inhibiting	Innovating
Rational	Intuitive
Exploring	Plodding
Perceiving	Judging
Extraverted	Intraverted
Left-Headed	Right-Headed
Theoretical	Practical
Controlling	Advising
Active	Passive
Technical	Social
Receptive	Perceptive
Formal	Informal
Team Player	Individual Contributor

Which type of categorization is best? Who knows? The purpose is to fit you into a job slot. But you do not want to think in terms of the job slots of the Industrial Society. You do not even want to think in terms of the new occupations which will replace the old occupations. In a few years they will be replaced by others that we do not yet have any ankling about.

Here is a tiny sample of, as yet, new occupations:

* Bionic medical technician

* Community ecologist

* Energy auditor

* Genetic counselor

* Nuclear medicine technologist

* Biotechnologist

* Software talent agent

* Space botanist

* Wellness consultant

* Learning tool developer.

Forget occupational categorizations. They are useful for gathering insights about you and possible occupations. But nothing more. Experts understand principles. But they do not understand the specific YOU.

Most experts are not as smart as you may believe. The story is told of Einstein's teacher telling Einstein that he would never be good at mathematics. Furthermore, Einstein was kicked out of Luitpold Gymnasium (a high school) and the principal told him:

> You seem skeptical about methods and subject matter.
> Your presence in the class undermines discipline.

You are unique. You may be categorized many different ways. You can spend a lifetime learning about yourself, something no expert would think of doing. And you can change. Everything depends upon you.

DON'T RELY ON TESTS

If not experts, how about tests? Aren't they objective? Do they not give you a fair assessment of your capabilities? No, they do not.

We live in a test-happy world. There are English tests, math tests, Regents tests, apptitude tests, and employment tests. We have IQ, SAT, LSAT, GRE, CBEST and hundreds of other alphabet-soup tests. And real estate exams, medical-practice exams, bar exams, teaching exams and so on and on and on and on. There are even tests for entering kindergarten!

Should you make decisions about your future based upon these tests? NO! NEVER! Most of these tests do not measure what they are supposed to be measuring. In addition they are not objective.

Let's look at the IQ (Intelligence Quotient) tests. IQ tests are highly biased by the format chosen, by the type of questions asked, and by the alternative answers presented. They are usually multiple-choice, which are easier to answer by some than be others, who may make out better in essay-type questions. The questions asked may favor one group of people above another.

Until about 1937, men received higher IQ test scores than women. At that time, the Stanford-Binet IQ test was adjusted to even out the outcomes between male and female test takers. How did they do this? They merely changed the questions until men and women test-takers received similar scores. Would you believe that this approach was called objective!

Today there are big differences in test scores between whites and blacks and other minorities, between high-income people and low-income people, and between the higher classes and the lower classes.

Furthermore, it is a well known fact that your emotional state has a strong influence over your performance on an IQ or any other standardized test. Some people have trouble taking tests.

Francine Patterson, a developmental psychologist, tells an interesting story about her work with a gorilla named Koko. She gave Koko IQ tests, and the gorilla scored a 95 and an 85, both in the average range. Actually, Patterson felt Koko should have gotten a better score. One question asked which of the following was best if you wanted to seek shelter from the rain: a hat, a spoon, a tree, or a house? Koko naturally chose *tree*, for which he was marked wrong. Patterson concludes that IQ tests exhibit

a cultural bias toward humans that show up when tests are administered to a gorilla.

Not only are tests biased, with coaching you can change your test results. Throughout the country there are coaching schools which enroll at least 50,000 students every year. For a price, these students learn how to take standardized tests by practicing taking tests. They review questions which have been used in previous tests, learn how to avoid pitfalls, and take advantage of flaws in the tests.

After concentrated coaching, those coached pull down better test scores. Lewis Pike, an employee of Educational Testing

Service, the largest test-maker in the country, did a study and wrote an internal memo in which he concluded that coaching could change scores on SAT by up to 13%.

In our society you may be required to take standardized tests. Study and receive the best coaching you can get to improve your score. Once you have taken the test and gotten a satisfactory score, forget it. The score should have NO bearing on your vision.

LISTEN TO YOUR "INNER VOICE"

But you may say, "I'm not a Gandhi, a King, a Jefferson, an Anthony, or an Einstein. I'm just an ordinary person trying to earn a living. Where will I find a vision?"

Your vision comes from within you. Somewhere inside you is a voice that is telling you what your vision should be. Follow it. If you can not hear your "inner voice", the great poet, Wordsworth, has some advice for you:

Look for the stars, you'll say that there are none;

Look up a second time, and, one be one,

You mark them twinkling out with silvery light

And wonder how they could elude the sight!

Look inside you to see what you want out of life. Look at your values, desires, and interests. What gets you excited? What turns you on? What do you enjoy doing more than anything else? What kind of job or activity would roll you out of bed before the sun is up and keep you tirelessly at it until after the moon is out? What do you think is important? What gives you that great expansive feeling of achievement? You have a vision in you. Look and you will find it.

LEARNING NUGGETS

The first vision principle is to Envision Your "Own Thing". The four rules for helping you do this are:

- **DON'T FOLLOW OTHERS—you may get lost**

- **DON'T RELY ON EXPERTS—they don't know YOU**
- **DON'T RELY ON TESTS—they are unreliable**
- **LISTEN TO YOUR "INNER VOICE"—it knows YOU.**

Chapter 4
Forget Mental Constraints

You have looked inside yourself and have visualized a fantastic vision. Now noisy doubts are fuzzying up your vision. Is my vision too grand? Do I have the character, capabilities, and mental capacity to achieve it? Will my mental weaknesses become obstacles? Perhaps I should lower my sights?

NO! Don't lower your sights.

Your so-called weaknesses can not prevent you from achieving what you desire. Besides your strengths are what shape you. Your strengths empower you. You can depend on them. But neither your weaknesses nor your strengths have as much impact upon your achievements as does your drive. If you have the will, the desire, the aspiration, you can live your vision.

No. Don't lower your sights. RAISE THEM!

Forget mental constraints. They are not obstacles. Follow these four rules:

- **Disregard Weaknesses**
- **Count on Your Strengths**
- **Depend on Your Drive**
- **Consider Sources of Help**

DISREGARD WEAKNESSES

There are at least two reasons why you should disregard your weaknesses. First, they probably are not true weaknesses. Second, even if they are, most of them can be overcome.

You Have Been Brainwashed

Most of us concentrate on our weaknesses. We dwell on our limitations and as a result limit our visions. We keep thinking of what we can't do, don't know, find hard to understand. Why?

Because the media are filled daily with negative stories of people whose strivings are beyond their reach. Robberies, hijackings, rapes, embezzlements, divorces, frauds, killings, treacheries, and swindles fill the airwaves. Rarely do the media present good, happy, and hopeful stories. There are many such stories, you know.

Because we have been brainwashed by schools, where teachers put children down and try to force them into intellectual straitjackets. Children come to school with wide-eyed curiosity and eagerness to learn. The first time they don't know the answer to a question, they are made to feel inferior. They are all given IQ and other tests, and those that do not get high grades are classified as slow learners or worse. Even those with good scores are often criticized for exercising initiative. Their self-image is quashed.

Because our families and friends are forever telling us what we can't or shouldn't do. As children we are told what is right, how to behave and how to do things. When we don't follow instructions and advice, we are frowned upon, sometimes punished. We grow up with a lot of negative feelings about what we can and can not do. Even when we are adults, our friends are always "reminding" us of our faults.

Deep down you know that much of the criticism you put up with is not true. And yet you say to yourself such things as:

* I'm not smart enough to be a physician

* I don't know enough mathematics to be an engineer

* I don't have the patience to be a teacher

* I don't have the talent to be an artist

* I am not observant enough to be a scientist

* I don't have the gumption to be a businessman.

These are what A.L Williams calls "failure messages". They are caused by labels given us by teachers, behavioral experts, parents, friends, schoolmates and colleagues. They are all around us. You and I know school classmates who were labeled "smart" but later in life could not make a living; and others who were labeled "stupid" who later became great achievers.

Many famous achievers did not have much formal schooling. Among them are:

* Henry Ford—founder of Ford Motor Company

* Wilbur and Orville Wright—inventors of the airplane

* Ansel Adams—one of the world's greatest photographers

* Harry Truman—president of the United States.

There is no correlation between doing well in school and achievement in industry or politics.

Replace negative labels drilled into your consciousness from outside with positive labels emanating from inside.

Weaknesses Can Be Overcome

Labels aside, if you are human you have mental weaknesses. But with some effort all the following basic mental capabilities can be improved:

OBSERVATION—Practice will inexorably improve your powers of observation.

MEMORY—The best way to improve your memory is to develop your ability to make associations. Memory expert Mort Herold says, "There are no poor memories.There are only untrained memories."

THINKING—The more you think, the better your thinking becomes. As Beverly-Coleene Galyean, who has been studying the brain, says, "The more we know, the more we can know."

CREATIVITY—Creativity is more than another way of thinking. It is an attitude. Are you curious and constantly seeking explanations? Do you ask questions or do you fall into the trap of following a well-worn script? Do you risk failure so you can learn? Scientist Roger Schank says that you can develop the creative attitude.

HUMAN RELATIONS—This is probably the most important capability you need. You must realize that you can become more skilled at it through study and practice. There are many books on human behavior on the market which may help.

No matter what type of intellectual weakness you have, you may overcome it with practice. Just as you improve your muscles through physical exercise, you enhance your mind through mental exercise.

COUNT ON YOUR STRENGTHS

Instead of dwelling on your weaknesses, concentrate on your strengths. Your strengths are the brushes with which you can paint your vision. Your strengths are the building blocks of your future design. Your strengths are what you are all about. You possess more strengths than you think. Be aware of them and know how to use them to your advantage.

You Can Do More Than You Think

Life is like a 10-speed bicycle. Most of us have gears that we never use.

So says Charles M. Schulz. And it's true. Just think about it. The very things you call weaknesses can be considered to be strengths, if viewed in a different light. A slow thinker may be called thorough because such a person usually spends a lot of time considering all the facts. At the other end is the person who is always jumping to conclusions, but perhaps she is intuitive. Then there is the undependable person, who should perhaps be labeled autonomous or an independent thinker. Someone called playful may also be creative.

Focusing on the negatives even if they are real, blinds you to your strengths. Take a look at the list of weaknesses I presented earlier. They can be rephrased positively as follows:

* Maybe not a physician, but I have the empathy to be a therapist

* Maybe not an engineer, but I have the visualization capability to be an architect

* Maybe not a teacher, but I have the verbal talent to be a writer

* Maybe not an artist, but I have the performance talent of an actor

* Maybe not a scientist, but I have the imagination of an inventor

* Maybe not a businessman, but I am skilled at human relations and can be a consultant.

Be Aware of Your Strengths

Forget about your weaknesses. Concentrate on your strengths. Joe Batten advocates that you make a long list of all your strengths because

You are the sum of your strengths.

To do this properly you need to know yourself. You need to face the age-old question: What sort of person am I? You have a lifetime to do this. But it would not hurt to start now. To undertand yourself better, it may be helpful to answer 3 questions:

WHAT ARE MY INTERESTS?—Am I interested in learning as much as possible in a specific area, or would I rather be a solver of problems or a creator? Do I want to be a specialist in a specific domain because I love this domain of knowledge and want to pursue the nitty-gritty details associated with it? Or do I want to be a problem solver because I do not care for detail, want to develop myself as a generalist, and get a keen sense of satisfaction from solving problems of any kind? Or do I want to be a creator because it allows me to be independent and innovative, and creating something new makes my soul sing?

WHAT IS MY PERSONAL ORIENTATION?—Do I like to work primarily with things, people, or ideas? Do I enjoy working with physical tools and tangible things? Or do I get my kicks from communicating, interacting, and socializing with people? Or would I rather spend my time hatching, comparing, and evaluating ideas?

WHAT ARE MY ABILITIES?—A product, a service, an intelligent service, any thing, any process, any idea has a life cycle. To which point in the life cycle are my abilities best suited? Am I a searcher, developer, builder, or fixer? Do I like to be at the forefront searching for what is new? Or a developer who takes what's new and makes it practical and useful? Or a builder who makes established things available to many people? Or a fixer who maintains and repairs things and ideas that have been in use for some time?

Think about yourself long and hard. Don't use the above questions as a means of classifying yourself. You can not be classified. These questions are only a way to open your mind to self exploration. You will think of many more questions to ask.

Another way to get to understand yourself, especially your strengths, is to write yourself a letter of recommendation. What is your vision? What are your interests? What sort of person are you? What qualities do you have that will enable you to achieve your desires? How can you be most useful to yourself? Put these down in the best letter you can write.

DEPEND ON YOUR DRIVE

So you study yourself and discover your major strenghts, and some major weaknesses. The weaknesses seem to you to be stumbling blocks, constraints upon your achieving your grand vision. At this point allow me to refer again to Albert Einstein. It sounds ridiculous to speak of mental constraints when talking about Albert Einstein. But listen to this statement made by Einstein when asked about his work:

> I think and think for months, for years. Ninety nine times the conclusion is false. The hundredth time I am right.

The man who is considered to be the greatest genius of the twentieth century, in effect said that persistence is more important than knowledge or brilliance in achieving what you want. If it's true for Einstein, it's definitely true for you and me. Why worry about mental constraints?

Forget about your limitations. It's your drive that counts. A team under the direction of Professor Benjamin Bloom, at the

University of Chicago, studied the lives of the top twenty Olympic swimmers, concert pianists, sculptors, tennis players, mathematicians and research neurologists. They found that in every case it was persistence—not so much talent—that made the person a star performer.

Abraham Lincoln presents an excellent example of the importance of drive. A.L. Williams lists all the defeats that Abraham Lincoln suffered:

* 1831   Failed in business

* 1832   Defeated for legislature

* 1833   Second failure in business

* 1836   Suffered nervous breakdown

* 1838   Defeated for speaker

* 1840   Defeated for elector

* 1843   Defeated for Congress

* 1848   Defeated for Congress

* 1855   Defeated for Senate

* 1856   Defeated for Vice President

* 1858   Defeated for Senate

But in

* 1860   Elected President of the United States.

Regardless of your strengths or your weaknesses, it is your drive that will enable you to live your vision.

Here is an example of what drive can do. Mark Wellman's dream was to climb mountains. But he was confronted with a huge drawback: he is a paraplegic, paralyzed from the waste down.

It did not stop him. In July of 1989, he climbed to the top of El Capitan, a 3500-foot-high rock in Yosemite in 8 days. With his climbing buddy, Mike Corbett, Wellman followed a path that was almost straight up. At one point Mike Corbett anchored a rope onto the Shelf Roof, a ledge that juts out 40 feet from the rock 2,000 feet above the valley floor. Wellman, who was hot and sweating from the 100-degree temperature produced by the blazing summer sun, who was blown by fierce winds as much as ten feet away from the rock, who received "a real pump" from peregrine falcons flying only 50 feet away from him sounding "like little jets," who could not use his legs for anything and who needed to depend on the upper part of his body only, pulled himself up at an agonizing *6 inches at a time*!

Since performing this and other feats, Wellman has enlarged his vision to helping other handicapped people define their visions in an unlimited way.

CONSIDER SOURCES OF HELP

Drive or not, in today's world it is impossible for you to know everything required for you to follow your vision. But you do not need to. More than ever before, it is easy for you to call on the talents, skills and resources of other people to help you. Also, high technology is at your service ready to raise your performance to levels you never thought possible.

Calling on People

The world is full of people who know different things. You may get their help by being part of a people network. Follow Socrates and ask questions. Begin dialogues and let them grow into discussions with several people. Expand your network. You can find the following people to help you:

THE COLLEAGUE—The colleague is in the same field as you. But she may be more knowledgeable or more skilled in certain tasks than you. You may indulge in dialogues and ask for help. You will get it if you do the same for your colleague.

THE COACH—A coach acts as a role model. She evaluates what you do and helps you change and improve. Coaches are useful for the development of talent and for the growing of difficult skills. The coach of a football team shows members what to do, builds up their confidence, and inspires the team to do its best. Similarly a mental coach inspires you by showing the way to solve a problem and then suggests improvements.

THE CATALYST—A catalyst is what Carl Rogers calls a learning facilitator. She sets the stage upon which the learning activity takes place. She invites you to where you can observe a process or activity. She builds a laboratory to encourage you to experiment. She has you indulge in role playing, simulations, and in playing games. A catalyst is different from a coach in the degree of interaction between you and her. A coach works together with you. A catalyst, once she sets the conditions for learning, leaves you more or less on your own.

THE COLLABORATOR—The collaborator is someone proficient in a different domain from yours. You work closely together to produce a product or an idea that neither of you could accomplish by himself. This is an example of synergy. You help each other for your mutual benefit.

THE CONTRIBUTOR—The contributor also is proficient in a different domain from yours. However, you do not work that closely together. She does her work and you do yours. Later you combine efforts.

Of course, there are many variations. The important thing to remember is that by building, maintaining, and nourishing your people network, you can get all the help you need.

Benefitting From Technology

Computer technology supplies you with learning tools to skyrocket your performance. Think of the computer as an intellectual outlet. We all have electrical outlets in our homes. Plug in a toaster and prepare a meal. Plug in an electrical power saw and build a cabinet. Plug in the TV and watch a show. With the computer, you can buy diskettes representing different programs for different tasks. Plug in a word-processing diskette and write a masterpiece. Plug in a graphics diskette and produce a work of art. Plug in a game diskette and play a game. Plug in learning tools and learn whatever you want to know.

Your computer may also extend your communications capability. It can stretch your people network to cover the globe.

When you consider what you can gain from your people network and from high technology—which is constantly expanding its power—instead of shrinking your vision because of what you think are mental constraints, you should expand your vision.

LEARNING NUGGETS

Don't get hung up on so-called mental constraints. Instead

- **DISREGARD WEAKNESSES—they can not stop you**
- **COUNT ON YOUR STRENGTHS—they empower you**
- **DEPEND ON YOUR DRIVE—it's what really counts**
- **CONSIDER SOURCES OF HELP—experts and tools can substitute for talent.**

Chapter 5

Affirm Your Values

What are values? How are values related to your vision? Why be concerned about values?

Values are concepts you prize. Values define how you live. Values are your reference points for making important decisions. Health. Love. Freedom. Security. Achievement. Honesty. Strength. These are some popular values.

I suggest that you list your values in order of their importance to you. Why? So you could get to know yourself better. So you could see that your vision and your values are in true harmony with each other. So you could be positive that the vision you are painting highlights what you truly are.

The above values are what I label personal values. They are concerned with your personal approach to living. But there are broader values, values showing your relationship to the many communities you are part of: economic, social, political and global. And you need these communities because

You can accomplish NOTHING by yourself.

You need people to achieve whatever you want, just as other people need you to achieve whatever they desire. This is why your vision should be good, not just for yourself, but for as many communities as possible. Moses knew this from the moment he saw the burning bush.

The recent drastic changes in technology is making community values, such as cooperation, community individualism, democracy and globalism come to the fore. To have a truly grand vision in our new society, you need to, not only be clear about your personal values, but also of your broader community values. You should:

- Foster Cooperation
- Give Intellectual and Emotional Support
- Build Participatory Democracy
- Be a Global Citizen

FOSTER COOPERATION

We've spent our lives imbued with the spirit of competition. We have been told that competition is the way to get ahead. Competition builds character and discipline. Competition places the best people on top. Competition is the route to becoming number one—a success.

As children we tried to show mommy and daddy we were better than our brothers and sisters. At school we studied for A's on the report card. After school hours, we struggled to be first in Little League. In college, we burned the midnight oil in pursuit of credentials, such as BSs, MBAs and PhDs, to hang in our offices or homes. In the corporation, we worked hard to please our superiors so that we could climb the ladder to the top. Corporation competed with corporation. Management competed with labor. One division competed with another division. Competition was an essential part of the Industrial Society.

It's impossible to remove competition from life. But to place it on a pedestal is ridiculous. Contrary to what we have been led to believe, almost none of the virtues attributed to competition is true, according to Alfie Kohn. In his book, *No Contest: The Case Against Competition,* Kohn presents the results of thousands of research reports, which prove that competition increases conformity, produces stress, increases aggression and cheating, degrades performance and decreases self-esteem.

In almost all competitions, you must conform to the goals and rules set up by someone else. In any one competition, most contestants lose. The result is a churning inside the stomachs of the rest of us.

If you doubt that competition increases aggression, just attend a sporting event. I remember taking my ten-year old son to see a hockey game. When he saw the contestants beating each other with their hockey sticks, he became white as a sheet and did not feel too good. We went to the bathroom. The sight here was worse. Several spectators had gotten into a fight. The loser was in the bathroom with a bloody nose.

Because it is impossible for the great majority of us to win, many of us resort to cheating. Scientists cheat in their research reports in order to get grants, defense contractors cheat the government to make more money, and cadets cheat at West Point to become officers. A college student recently wrote a book called *Cheating 101*, a manual of different ways to cheat on an exam.

Competition does not improve, but degrades, performance. We enter a contest, not to do our very best, but to win the approval of other people.But we perform best, not when pulled by external rewards, but when pushed by our own drives. Because we feel we are not at our best we compete more and more and are not reassured. Whether we win or lose, we lose our self-esteem.

Competition is a separator of people.Cooperation is an integrator of people. It:

INCREASES INDIVIDUALITY—Cooperation decreases conformity and allows each of us to contribute in her own way.

REDUCES STRESS—Cooperation reduces stress since we no longer spend all our time trying to impress people.

DECREASES AGGRESSION—Cooperation, unlike competition, does not make us aggressive and eager to challenge anyone who disagrees with us or who thinks differently from us. We try to help, and everyone loves a helper.

DECREASES CHEATING—Cooperation provides no incentive to cheat: we are all working toward the same goal.

ENHANCES PERFORMANCE—Cooperation yields group performance which is greater than can be achieved by any one of us working alone.

ENHANCES SELF-ESTEEM—Cooperation causes each of us to rise in our own self-esteem because we have contributed to the excellence of the group.

Putting cooperation on your list of community values is bound to enhance your vision.

GIVE INTELLECTUAL AND EMOTIONAL SUPPORT

You need to cooperate with people in many communities:

* ECONOMIC—Employees, colleagues, customers, vendors, stockholders, savers, competitors, clients, advisors, and society members

* SOCIAL—Family, friends, neighbors, teachers, and members of organizations (social, ethnic, racial, educational, and religious)

* POLITICAL—Police, legal, government benefits, military, voting, party, self-interest group, and public-interest group

* GLOBAL—Economic, social, political, environmental, and volunteer.

Think of yourself as an individual at the center of a complex web of relationships. You are an individual, yes. But what you do impacts a great number of individuals. What these individuals do impacts you.

You Need People.

You need people, not only to help you accomplish your objectives, but also for support. You need them for networking, something you must do to find clients, customers, employment, partners, intellectual stimulation, and ideas and techniques to test. You need them for friendship, love, support, recreation, companionship, and joy.

The people running the Manville Corporation thought they did not need other people. On August 26, 1982, the chairman and CEO of this company, the biggest producer of asbestos in this country, filed for bankruptcy. Was the company in the red? No, it had $2 billion dollars in assets. Was it losing market share? No, it was 181 on the Fortune 500 list. What was wrong? The company faced 16,500 lawsuits and was expecting the total number of lawsuits to increase to 52,000. Why? Because for five decades the company hid the fact from its employees that exposure to asbestos may cause lung cancer and asbestosis, a crippling lung diseaser. The chairman said the company was filing for bankruptcy to avoid paying all these claims. He did not then, nor did he consider before, the needs of his most important community: his employees.

Contrast this story about Manville with the way Johnson and Johnson acted in the Tylenol scare. On February 8, 1986, Diane Elsroth of Peekskill, New York, who was only 23, died after swallowing 2 Extra Strength Tylenol capsules. Evidently someone had laced the capsules with potassium cyanide. Immediately Chairman James Burke of Johnson and Johnson, the company that manufactures Tylenol, said the company will no longer sell capsules of Tylenol over the counter. He made this statement:

> We take this action with great reluctance and a heavy heart. But since we can't control random tampering with capsules after they leave our plant, we feel we owe it to consumers to remove capsules from the market.

It's been estimated that recalling all the products and scrapping production cost the company about $150 million. But Johnson and Johnson evidently has a vision which includes its customer community. A few months after the incident, Johnson and Johnson was selling what are called caplets of Tylenol in tamper-proof bottles. The company regained most of its market! People appreciated the company's integrity, an integrity which sprang from its vision.

People Need You.

The best vision satisfies a need of people. It seems pointless to do anything which does not help some people, somewhere in some way. Helen Keller, the world-renowned blind person of great achievement, said:

> Life is an exciting business and most exciting when lived for others.

Include your communities in your vision.

BUILD PARTICIPATORY DEMOCRACY

We, in the United States, have had democracy in our political affairs and in our social affairs for a long time. But not in our economic affairs. The typical corporation is a dictatorship. This, however, is changing.

Economic democracy is coming via the team concept; forming teams of workers who manage their own affairs is one of the best ways to improve the quality of products and services. It is coming via limited employee voting—at companies such as at Donnelly Mirrors, team members vote to elect representatives to committees that represent them. It is coming via "open book" companies—at organizations such as NeXt, each employee has access to the most confidential information. It is coming via employee ownership—at companies such as Marion Labs and Dana Corporation, each employee is an owner.

Through the efforts of a few visionaries we are discovering that democracy definitely makes for a more cohesive community. When you know you have a voice in what happens you are more interested in affecting results. You feel like working harder because it is something you have decided is important. Because all of you in the group have had discussions and have taken common action you all feel like cooperating with each other for the common good.

Participatory democracy is growing in the corporation. It is a community value you may use to embellish your vision.

BE A GLOBAL CITIZEN

We all believe in good citizenship as a community value. I like to express the idea of citizenship this way:

Pursuing happiness while supporting a healthy nation

In the past, a nation has been considered healthy if it is healthy economically, socially and politically. But the building of our industrial economy has caused a pell-mell exploitation of the Earth's physical resources. Our natural resources are being depleted at a catastrophic rate. Our physical environment is being polluted to the point of hazard. Our economy is bringing us suffocating materialism and consumerism, which is ruining the social and political health of the nation. Octavio Paz, who was awarded the 1990 Nobel Prize for Literature, says:

> The question of the market is intricately related to the deterioration of the environment. Pollution affects not only the air, the rivers, and the forests, it also affects our souls. A society possessed by the frantic need to produce more in order to consume more tends to reduce ideas, feelings, art, love, friendship, and people themselves to consumer products. Everything becomes a thing to be bought, used, and thrown on the rubbish heap. No other society has produced so much waste, material and moral, as ours.

To be a good citizen today, you must consider how your actions affect, not only the economic, social and political health of the nation, but also its environmental health. But our environment and the environments of other nations are intimately related. As a matter of fact, all aspects of our nation's health and the health of other nations on the Globe are interrelated. A few examples:

* American fossil-fuel burning plants and vehicles pollute the air with sulphur and nitrogen oxides, and the winds take them to Canada to produce acid rain

* We sell to El Salvador DDT, which poisons the water and kills fish, birds and other animals. To avoid starvation, El Salvadorans become illegal immigrants to the United States

* In Columbia, addictive drugs are cash crops. When they export these drugs to the United States, it causes drug addiction and crime. In this case, we declare war on drugs, which results in drug lords terrorizing the people in Columbia

* An American, driving a Japanese car, has a leak in her air conditioning unit. The Freon gas rises up to the stratosphere and three years later helps rip appart the ozone layer over the Southern Hemisphere. Since the ozone layer protects people from ultra violet radiation, a rip in it gives cancer to an individual at the tip of Argentina when he goes swimming.

The Globe is one. What happens on one side of the Globe affects what happens on the other side of the Globe.

What does all this mean? It means that our definition of citizenship must be expanded. We must be Global Citizens. A Global Citizen is one who:

> pursues happiness while supporting a healthy nation
> as part of a healthy Globe.

Because the world is one, all nations around the Globe are interdependent economically, socially, politically and environmentally. Because the world is one, competition among nations is destructive to all of us. Because the world is one, cooperation among nations is the only path to follow to make the Globe and all the nations on the Globe healthy.

Global citizenship should be one of your important community values.

LEARNING NUGGETS

Affirm your values, especially your community values:

- **FOSTER COOPERATION—it brings better results than competition**

- **GIVE INTELLECTUAL AND EMOTIONAL SUPPORT—it elicits the power of the individual**

- **BUILD PARTICIPATORY DEMOCRACY—it allows individual creativity to contribute to our common good**

- **BE A GLOBAL CITIZEN—to save our Globe.**

Chapter 6

Make it a Movie - Not Snapshots

All the world's a stage,

   And all the men and women merely players,

   They have their exits and their entrances;

   And one man in his time plays many parts

So said the great Shakespeare. And it's true. Life is a big show. Life is not a series of achievements:

* not following a plan consisting of goals—snapshots—but a MOVIE

* not a series of victories—sculptures—but a DRAMA

* not enjoying many wonderful pleasures—melodies—but a SYMPHONY.

Your vision is the script of your movie, the theme of your drama, the enchantment of your symphony. Your vision is your guide as an actor, performer and player. Your vision is the most important thing about you. It *is* you because

YOU are the

AUTHOR, STAR, DIRECTOR, AUDIENCE, and CRITIC of your own show.

Make it magnificent!

Specifically,

* **Don't Focus on Goals**

Instead

- **Write a Full-Length-Life Movie**
- **Run Your Own Drama**
- **Critique Your Unfinished Symphony**

DON'T FOCUS ON GOALS

A vision is not a product, a service, a system, an organization, a skill, a prize, an award, or a situation that can be achieved. A vision is not a goal. Nor is it a plan, a roadmap, a schedule; or a method for time management, work organization, or team-leading which may be used to achieve a goal.

Almost everyone who writes a book about how you can be a success, speaks of goal setting and planning. Set your main goal, and then set many subgoals, they state. And then every day have a TO-DO list to follow to assure you are making progress. Avoid procrastination and keep on top of your goals and lists and you will reach the top and become the best, a winner, number one.

I don't agree. I object to this absorption, fascination, and engulfment with goal setting. I am not against goal setting as a technique. It definitely does have utility. Goal setting is a good way of focusing yourself on a job to be done.

I set goals. One of my goals was to write this book. But I did not set this goal because I thought it would make me number one in literature (practically impossible), or that it would make me a winner (with whom am I competing?) Why did I decide to write this book? Because it conforms to my vision of spreading the word about future design and visions. If you have a vision, you don't have to worry about choosing goals to achieve. Your vision makes your major goals obvious.

A goal is not the same as a vision.

A goal is merely a snapshot, an event, a temporary achievement. A vision is a movie, a process, a guide of your entire life. Many of us have often confused materialistic, evanescent goals with intellectual, long-lasting visions.

* Making a million dollars is a *goal*. It is not a vision. A VISION would be designing the most comfortable homes you are capable of.

* Becoming president of a company is a *goal*. It is not a vision. A VISION would be making the power of computers available to the masses.

* Winning an Olympic competition is a *goal*. It is not a vision. A VISION would be to use competitive sports as a means of making the world a more peaceful place.

* Becoming president of the United States is a *goal*. It is not a vision. A VISION would be to remove as much corruption as possible in public life.

I am not against planning and scheduling. Breaking up a big goal into smaller sub-goals to which you assign completion dates helps you get the job done on time. Often it may be the only way to get it done at all. For this book, I developed a plan and a writing schedule, which helped me tremendously.

A plan is a way for achieving your defined goals which conform to your vision. Failing to reach a goal does not make you a failure, providing you live according to your vision. You set yourself another goal and work towards that. When I started this book, I made a schedule showing when it would be completed and when it would be published. I did not achieve either goal. So what? I revised the book several times until finally it was published. Planning and scheduling are necessary for big projects, but the important thing is to follow your vision.

I am not against TO-DO lists either. They are useful in jogging your memory and keeping you focused. But I don't believe that becoming a slave to a TO-DO list will make you perform better or achieve more. Suppose an opportunity that is not on your TO-DO list hits you in the eyes. What do you do? Forget it and follow your TO-DO list?

TO-DO lists are useful time-management tools. But they should not guide your behavior. Your actions should be guided by your vision.

A good example of the difference between goals (snapshots) and visions (movies) is given by a former president of the United States: Jimmy Carter. He had a goal of becoming president of the United States, and he achieved it. But his vision was something more. He wanted to promote human rights, human health, and human peace around the Globe.

While Carter was president, he pushed human rights around the world as much as he could. One of his major achievement was the Camp David accords between Israel and Egypt, which brought peace between these two long-warring countries. But he lost the next presidential election to Ronald Reagan.

Carter did not meet his goal. Does this mean he was a failure? Of course, not. It's true that he did not succeed in reaching his goal of being reelected. But his vision remained with him. He sold his peanut warehouse and, with $27 million he and his wife raised through donations, established the Carter Center. This is not another presidential library, but as the New York Times Magazine says:

> a think tank and 'conflict resolution' hub, the center is sort of a vest pocket World Health Organization, miniature UN and ad hoc Department of Health and Human Services.

Yes, he kept his vision of spreading democracy and respect for human rights throughout the world. He was the most respected monitor of the Nicaragua election which brought democracy to the beleaguered country and gave Violeta Chamorro her orderly election victory. He was an observer in talks between Ethiopia's communist government and the northern rebels. He and former president Gerald Ford monitored elections in Panama and confronted that government with evidence of massive fraud.

In addition to these activities, Jimmy Carter sponsors the Annual Jimmy Carter Work Project. Volunteers from all over the world come to a poor area, live in tents without running water, and build homes for poor people.

Though he lost the election, Carter's popularity has since then zoomed. He failed to reach a goal, but he is living according to his vision.

WRITE A FULL-LENGTH-LIFE MOVIE

No. Life is not a snapshot or a series of snapshots. It is not a slide show which gives a staccato presentation of events. It is not a mish-mash of all the things that may happen to you. Life is a continuous process and your vision should be about your life as a whole.

When planning their lives, many people think of stepping stones to their destination, or wrungs of a ladder that leads to their destiny. They think of their lives as a sequentially-phased series of achievements leading to their supreme achievement. They plan a series of mini-newsreels, each more fulfilling than the previous one.

One form this takes is what Richard N. Bolles calls the three boxes of life. During the first third, they go to school to become educated. In the second third, they work to make money. In the last third, they have fun and relax. The working box is often subdivided further.

You know these people. They are building up their resumes. They take an uninspiring job because it may lead to another more important job, which in turn may lead to a still higher job. Eventually—they hope it won't be too late—they may qualify for the job of their dreams.

Dividing your life into boxes this way strikes Bolles, as it does me, as being dull. Instead of snapshots or newsreels, envision your life as a full-length movie. Make your movie dramatic and interesting by combining learning, work and leisure throughout your life.

Don't build your resume. Follow your vision!

YOU write the script for this full-length-life movie. What an opportunity you have! You can write a script that presents YOUR values, YOUR philosophy, YOUR interests, YOUR ideas, YOUR needs. No censorship. No arguments. No compromises.

You are the AUTHOR.

What a vision you can make it. Look at the movie that Moses made. The movie was so interesting it was repeated in modern times and portrayed by Charlton Heston, a performance that made him a star.

Your vision can be a dramatic presentation of your complete life, your life as a whole. Write a beautiful script.

RUN YOUR OWN DRAMA

Life is not a sculpture or a series of sculptures, but a drama. When you write the script of your vision remember:

You Are the STAR.

Do the best you know how. Ad lib for the most part. Of course you have the script you wrote. But the script presents only the big picture. You have a chance to experiment, learn, and innovate. Try new roles. Develop fresh ideas. Enjoy what you do.

Enjoy your work as well as your learning and your leisure activities. The grandest vision is one which you are sure you will enjoy pursuing. You will do your best, and you will reap the highest rewards. What a vision you have if you can do your work without concern for money or fame, but because you enjoy it. Kenyon Cox expressed this thought well:

> Work thou for pleasure—paint, or sing, or carve
>
> The thing thou lovest, though the body starve -
>
> Who works for glory misses oft the goal;
>
> Who works for money coins his very soul.
>
> Work for the work's sake, then, and it may be
>
> That these things shall be added unto thee.

You Are the DIRECTOR.

Like any star you need guidance at times. You need a director to show you how to play certain roles, maybe even provide you with a plan. No problem. You are the director, the one to develop the plan to enable you to play your part better.

As a director, you have a steady job, because nothing in life stands still. People change. Technology changes. Organizations change.The physical environment changes. The intellectual environment changes. It's this constant change that gives life its exuberance. It causes you to spend a lifetime learning. Your learning enables you to play a better role.

A smart director always looks for ways to improve the star's acting. Sometimes, your learning indicates that you should change your starring role. Why not? Your learning may enable you to enhance your vision. This is why your vision should be open ended and flexible. Why not? Occasionally your learning may encourage you to completely change your vision. Why not? It's your show. Enjoy it.

You Are the AUDIENCE.

You are not only the star and the director. You are the audience. When you write the script of your vision, ask yourself a few questions. Would you want to sit through and watch such a performance? Would you like the performance? Would you enjoy it? Would you cheer in the right places?

Make it a powerful drama that even YOU would be proud of.

CRITIQUE YOUR UNFINISHED SYMPHONY

Life is not a melody or a series of melodies, but a symphony. Not only are you the composer and star violinist, you are your own conductor, audience and reviewer. Write a symphony that you will enjoy, be enthralled with, that will excite you, that you can give rave reviews about, that you will feel like recommending to others.

You are the CRITIC.

Be tough on yourself. This is the only way to make your vision grand and your life as fulfilling as possible. Socrates long ago remarked that:

> The life which is unexamined is not worth living.

Examine your vision often. Don't compare it with the vision or performance of anyone else. You are not in competition with anyone. You want to always do the best you are capable of—for your own satisfaction.

Do YOU hear the music? Do YOU like it?

Your symphony, your vision, has no end, no specific point after which people rise and applaud. A vision is not something attainable in the sense that you feel, at some point, a sense of completion. Goals are attainable. Looked at in this way, a vision is an unattainable, or ideal, goal. Moses had the vision of making his people a great nation. Being a great nation is an ideal. A nation can always become greater than it is. A vision is a never-ending quest for the ideal.

Franz Peter Schubert, the great composer, wrote many songs and symphonies. The Eighth Symphony in B Minor is considered by many musical experts to be one of his best, even though it appears to be unfinished. This Unfinished Symphony may be unfinished in a formal sense, but it still brings joy and inspiration to people all over the world.

Make your vision one that will guide you to a full self-actualized life, one where at the end you will be wanting more.

Make your vision an unfinished symphony.

LEARNING NUGGETS

To write a script for a happy self-actualized life:

- **DON'T FOCUS ON GOALS—being a TO-DO-list slave limits you**

- **WRITE A FULL-LENGTH-LIFE MOVIE—think of life as an interesting whole**

- **RUN YOUR OWN DRAMA—make life zesty by enjoying what you do, doing what you enjoy and always learning**

- **CRITIQUE YOUR UNFINISHED SYMPHONY— die still trying to improve your vision.**

SECTION II

LEARNING

To Achieve Your Vision

Chapter 7

The Learning Society

Having a grand vision is not enough. Sure your vision will motivate you. But motivation is not enough either. Motivation may get you excited and committed and thinking positively. But how long can you sustain this feeling? Until the next motivation session?

I like to compare motivation sessions to diets. When a lady finds a diet and follows the instructions closely, she loses thirty pounds. She looks stunning, feels great and possesses a positive outlook. But after a time, she reverts to her old eating habits and gains her thirty pounds back. Her looks deteriorate, she becomes depressed and develops a negative outlook. So she searches for another diet. The lady goes up and down like a yo-yo.

Isn't the salesman who periodically attends motivational sessions just like the diet-crazy lady? As soon as he loses his "motivation" he comes to the motivational speaker to get a "shot" so he could once more be "motivated".

You need more than motivation. You need action, the kind of action that supports your vision, the kind that leads to learning—such as that done by

SOCRATES

A story is told about Socrates, the son of a stone cutter, who even in his youth was curious and asked lots of questions. One day Socrates went with his boyhood friend, Crito, to visit Mouse, the potter. The two boys stared in amazement as Mouse fashioned a piece of clay slowly and carefully and with small almost unnoticed movements of his hands and fingers into a beautiful

pitcher. Socrates, who was considered by some to be physically
ugly, began the dialogue with Mouse:

> Beautiful. What does beautiful mean?

>> This pot is beautiful. But not this one that I did
>> yesterday. I spoiled it.

> No, Mouse. That's what people always do—point at
> things. People talk about beautiful pots, beautiful
> people, beautiful ideas. What is *the* beautiful?

>> I don't know about *the* beautiful. I only know about
>> pots. A good pot is beautiful to me.

> But why is it good?

>> See that pitcher. It is good for something. It is good
>> for pouring. Make the lip more deeply curved and the
>> wine will spill. A good pitcher does what it's supposed
>> to do well.

> Why doesn't everybody make good pitchers?

>> They don't know how. They don't know what the
>> pattern of a good pitcher is.

> But who made the pattern?

>> Not me. Not my father. It took a long time. We're still
>> making changes. Perhaps the real pattern isn't made
>> at all. It goes on being discovered.

> Then how do you discover it?

>> I'm not sure I know. But first you must know pitchers.
>> You must know what it is in them that makes them
>> good pitchers. You must know. You must learn.

Socrates learned and helped other people learn by asking
questions. He was not so much concerned with pitchers and pots
as he was with ideas. He was searching for the meaning of beauty,
goodness, truth. He was searching for knowledge and enjoyed
helping others reach understanding.

Civilization forgot about Socrates. Especially in the Industrial
Society. We focused on pitchers and pots. We made pots by the
millions. We built complicated machinery so that we could build
more pots. We set up a school system to authoritatively educate
children about pots: how to design pots, how to improve the

chemistry and physics of clay to produce better pots, how to engineer more efficient machinery for making pots, how to sell pots, how to manage workers so that they make good pots, and how to make money from pots.

When the computer arrived we switched from pots to pot-related services. Within the company, experts trained the rest of us to realize the value of pots: how to improve the quality of pots, how to be committed to producing the best pots, how to get along with people you hate in order to be proud of your pots, how to make sure customers love your pots. Outside the company, experts, sport celebrities and other pundits gave more impassioned presentations with titles such as:

* Why Pitchers and Pots Make the World a Better Place to Live In

* Beauty of Pots—from Socrates to Modern Times

* The Future of Pot-Making Technology

* If I Can Hit a Home Run, You Can Sell More Pots.

It wasn't until very recently that we finally remembered Socrates. After our preoccupation with pots and pontificating on pots we now prefer people. We are now concentrating on people learning. Specifically, we may think of this transformation in our thinking in terms of three steps:

- **Education by Authorities**
- **Training by Experts**
- **Learning by People**

EDUCATION BY AUTHORITIES

Our educational system has supported our industrial system, which is an outgrowth of the physical sciences.

The physical sciences got their great boost from Francis Bacon, who propounded the scientific method. The scientific method consists of four steps:

HYPOTHESIS—a statement that may explain all of the facts related to a natural phenomenon.

DEDUCTION—a statement, that can be logically deduced from the hypothesis, which can be proven true or false.

OBSERVATION & EXPERIMENT—a look at the real world to see if the deduction is true.

CONCLUSION—if the results prove the deduction correct, it tends to prove the hypothesis.

The four steps are in reality a loop that is repeated over and over. A hypothesis is chosen based on an inductive process that considers all the relevant facts derived from previous objective experiments and observations. Many observations and experiments are needed to increase confidence in a hypothesis.A successful hypothesis becomes a theory and eventually, if no negative results are found, a law.

Once this new method for learning was understood and adopted, scientific investigations began to flower and thrive. Isaac Newton gave us the Law of Gravity, which later helped us shoot satellites into orbit for world-wide communication. James Clerk Maxwell and Heinrich Hertz, among many others, laid the groundwork for radio and television. The experiments of Antoine Laurent Lavoisier made him the father of chemistry. He and his many followers gave us a rich variety of chemicals, glues, pastes, medicines, gasolene, plastics and special materials. Thomas Edison applied the scientific method to the invention of the light bulb and electricity. From his work and the work of the many inventors that followed him, we now have can openers, cooking and cooling and heating systems, dishwashers, electric shavers, garbage disposers, hair-curling irons, lamps, refrigerators, power tools, and the gadget-of-the-week.

The study of physical sciences led to technology and to the mass production of physical goods by big highly-structured corporations. The school of the Industrial Society was similarly structured. The corporation defined its job slots: blue collars to tend the machines, white collars for the more intellectually-demanding tasks. And the school supplied the people for these slots: vocational schools for the blue collars and colleges for the white collars. To let the corporation know what slot to put a person in, the school supplied each graduate with a credential: BS, MBA, PhD.

In the school of the Industrial Society:

* the students were obedient and orderly
* students learned through memorization and recitation
* some subjects were taught by drill and practice
* students crammed in order to pass tests
* the main purpose for students was to get a degree, to prove they were "educated".

TRAINING BY EXPERTS

When the computer arrived, it revolutionized the corporation. Things changed so rapidly within the corporation, that it could no longer depend upon the educational system. And so began corporate training.

The Revolutionary Computer

Von Neumann, a mathematician, is credited with the invention of the computer, which is often called a Von Neumann machine. He designed it for mathematical calculations. But like Galileo's telescope which opened a window on the physical universe, the computer flung open an expanding window to an entirely new conceptual universe: the mind.

What is a *computer*? It is unlike any invention that preceeded it. It is not merely a communication device like the telephone, radio, television set, VCR and CD player. Nor is it only a device for performing calculations. The computer is more powerful than any tool our civilization has developed. Implications stemming from this super-tool are profound.

To appreciate its significance, let us compare the computer with the electronic calculator. With a calculator, you the user put in numbers, hit an operator key which causes the calculator to produce a result, then enter other numbers and hit other operator keys to produce other results. You continue until the problem is solved. In other words, you and the calculator work together to solve the problem.

With a computer, the process is entirely different. You enter a series of instructions representing the above sequence together with all the data, and the computer does everything. You can use this sequence of instructions—a *program*—over and over again with new batches of data.

The concept is more radical than it appears at first glance. Think about it. We ask the machine to reproduce the steps of an intellectual task.The machine does this by building another world where electrons run around to accomplish what we ask. In essence, the computer imitates with its electrons what we do when we solve a problem. This means that if we can think of a procedure, not only for solving a mathematical problem but for doing anything, we can get the computer to do it for us fa-a-a-a-a-ster! Thus we can get the computer to store away data and search and retrieve when we need it—a fast Rolodex. Or we can get the computer to sequence through the procedures for drawing a house. Or we can make the computer go through procedures simulating the operation of a machine, a system, a corporation, a war, or a world of fantasy limited only by our imagination.

The computer and its offspring unleashed a flood of information systems which transformed the corporation. An *information system* is more than a communication system. It is a means of organizing data in such a way that the resultant information makes it easier for the recipient to make decisions and solve problems. Thus we developed data base management systems, management information systems, computer-aided instruction systems, and many more.

Corporate Training

The analysis of operations that is required before designing information systems led to greater understanding of the corporation. This led to restructuring of the corporation, to the development of work teams, to the acquisition of new technology, to the redifinition of management. These gut-wrenching changes wrought havoc in the corporation.

Because the educational establishment could not keep up with the changes, companies have developed training programs of their own. The training programs were designed by experts to:

* introduce new technology

* explain the redesign of the organizational structure

* introduce new techniques of management

* help develop a new culture befitting the new environment.

LEARNING BY PEOPLE

The materialistic Industrial Society has collapsed, just as the Agricultural Society had collapsed before it. At one time agriculture occupied 90% of the working population. Today it uses 2-1/2%. At its height, manufacturing (if you include the necessary distribution and retailing) occupied the vast majority of the workforce. In 1985 it was down to 19% of the workforce. It is estimated that in the year 2000 it will provide work for only 9%.

Economists tell us that the service sector is replacing the production sector as the major source of employment. In 1985, 75% of all workers in the United States were in the service sector. According to economist Robert Hamrin, only 2% of these workers were in personal services, such as barbershops and restaurants. The implication is that most of these workers are in mental services—such as law, medicine, finance, tax preparation, nutrition consulting, management consulting, architecture, environmental consulting, human-relationships advising, drug-addiction advising, researching, inventing. The trend is, not to low-paying physical services, but to high-paying intelligent services.

Data, Information, and Knowledge

Most of us believe that to perform intelligent services, we need lots of information. This is not true. We need more than information; we need knowledge. Because the terms data, information and knowledge are often used interchangeably, I want to explain the differences among them before proceding:

DATA—Simple statements of fact, such as "Jane has red hair," "Today is Sunday," and "The table is six feet long".

INFORMATION—Data organized to simplify communication:

* Tables of characteristics

* Summarization of accounts

* Report on a market study

* Answer to a specific request

* Book on leadership..

Information flows from person to person, or from person via machine to person. It's purpose is to help a person make a decision.

KNOWLEDGE—This is information that has been aggregated to its highest level inside the mind. It is the stuff of decision-making, unique to each individual. Knowledge does not come from any source outside ourselves. Each of us gathers experience and information and uses them to grow knowledge in his mind. As Thomas A. Dwyer, of the University of Pittsburgh, puts it, "No knowledge is really transmitted; it must all be created."

Here are a few examples which distinguish information from knowledge:

* A telephone directory, which lists all the names, addresses and telephone numbers in a city is *information;* rules a person has for using this information in a telemarketing program are KNOWLEDGE

* A daily newspaper supplies economic *information*; the economist, who understands current economic events, possesses KNOWLEDGE

* A list of the Hollywood Oscar winners is *information;* Dustin Hoffman, who understands how to win an Oscar, possesses KNOWLEDGE.

Learning: The Growing of Knowledge

The distinction between information and knowledge is related to the distinction between communication and learning. To see this clearly, let's look at what happens when you talk to your friend. You have knowledge in your mind, learned from long years of experience.When you communicate with her you convert your knowledge into language that she may understand:

information. When this information reaches your friend, she associates it with other items in her mind to develop her own knowledge—she's learning.

Socrates showed the way to learning. Socrates did not teach or train. He did not impart information. Socrates indulged in a dialogue with another person so that both he and and his partner could build their knowledge together. They both learned.

Dialogue is controlled by the individual. The big difference between teaching and training on one hand and learning on the other, is this: Teaching and training are done by other people. Learning is done by you

Learning is not a thing. It is not something you can pick up, receive, get, have, give. It is not something you find in books. You can't buy it anywhere. Learning takes place in your mind.

We are not living in the Information Society, but in THE LEARNING SOCIETY. So says none other than my famous namesake, Jonathan Livingston Seagull:

> I don't care what they say. There's so much more to flying than just flapping around from place to place. A...a....mosquito does that! One little barrel-role around the Elder Gull, just for fun, and I'm an Outcast! Are they blind? Can't they see? Can't they think of the glory that it'll be when we really learn to fly?

If you want to be able to "fly", here are principles to guide your learning:

- **Seek Knowledge—Not Information**
- **Take Risks for Creativity**
- **Direct Your Own Learning**
- **Make Learning a Lifetime Habit.**

Each is discussed in a succeeding chapter in this section.

Chapter 8

Seek Knowledge—Not Information

Knowledge is not something you have. You are not born with it. There is no place you can go to get it. There is no expert around that can give it to you. You can't find it in books. You can't get it from the media. You can't buy it in any store.

You may do all of these things with information, but not with knowledge. Information comes from without; knowledge comes from within. Information reaches you through the media; knowledge you grow in your mind. The nature and type of information you receive is determined by the sender; the nature and type of knowledge you grow is determined by YOU.

Learning is the process of growing knowledge in your mind. It is the process whereby you relate your experiences and the information you gather from all sources to produce a mental framework that guides all your activities. Excellent learners are not busy gathering information as much as they are comparing, analyzing, synthesizing the information they have into a coherent whole. Excellent learners are busy solving problems.

To become an effective learner:

- **Don't Be an Information Sponge**

Instead follow the I-D-E-A loop in pursuit of knowledge:

- **I—Inquire and Dialogue**
- **D—Do and Experiment**
- **E—Evaluate and Conclude**
- **A—Amend and Try Again**

DON'T BE AN INFORMATION SPONGE

Every place you go you are inundated with information. When you talk to your spouse, sweetheart, friends. When you use the telephone and fax machine. When you read the newspaper. When you go shopping. When you are in your car listening to talk shows.

At work you are submerged in a sea of information. Undoubtedly you have an information system at work. Computers spew out reams of reports. Communication systems tie you to anyone in the world. Desktop presentation systems display the information to make a lasting impression. You attend meetings to hear words of wisdom and to get you excited about your work. Do you need all this information?

Do you listen to talk shows? Lots of good stories. Immediate solutions to the most complex problems. Lots of information.

How about TV? Television is the disseminator of information par excellence. It demonstrates that if you buy product X you will be more attractive to the opposite sex, and if you buy product Y it will boost your self esteem. Ra. Ra. Ra. You get the latest information about who was killed yesterday. How pretty the burning homes in the hills look. Which movie star was divorced, got himself a new wife, or is opening in the most exciting movie of all time. The latest spin about the president's gaffes from governors, senators and other politicians. Even important fifteen-second announcements of the president. This is called *news*.

Information. Do you need it? Oh, you say, I want to be well informed. A friend of mine told me the other day that he reads the daily newspaper from cover to cover. He was talking about the Los Angeles Times, each issue of which may consist of 10 to 20 pounds of paper.

I think that reading the newspaper—a good one—is a good way to keep track of the news. But the entire paper? What on earth for? You don't want to be *well informed*. You want to be KNOWLEDGEABLE. You want to understand what's happening. When you read the paper, pick and choose the subjects that are important to you, not those important to the editor. This is the main reason I prefer a newspaper to the radio or TV: it is very easy to disregard the hustlers, the fluff and what does not interest me.

You are in the pursuit of knowledge, not the gathering of information.

I—INQUIRE AND DIALOGUE

Our experiences are filled with things that we do not understand. This is why we need to ask questions and initiate dialogues. We ask questions of friends, associates, colleagues, bosses, experts—anyone who may have the answer. We ask questions of books. We ask questions of nature. Albert Einstein's primary skill was the ability to ask original questions. As a young boy, each day Isaac Isador Rabi, the budding eminent physicist, came home from school, his mother asked him:

Did you ask any good questions today, Isaac?

But dialogue is more than asking questions. The other side of the dialogue is listening. Most of us do not listen carefully. We are busy judging, warning, preaching, advising, persuading, ordering, praising, ridiculing, interpreting, reassuring or kidding.

Good listening means determining the purpose of what is said and the logic supporting the statements. It means figuring out the assumptions made, including those that are not stated. A good listener hears the body language. She notices the shifting eyes and the nervous walking.

Good listening leads to good understanding and to excellent rapport.

What you can't get through dialogue or discussion, you may search for. But search only for information that is significant, that is, information that helps you in your mental processes.

D—DO AND EXPERIMENT

Questioning and listening do not suffice. You need to do something. You need to experiment with new ideas, approaches, concepts. You need to solve problems.

How do you learn a skill, such as riding a bicycle? By asking questions? This is hardly enough. You may learn about the theory. But to actually learn how to do it, you must get onto the bicycle and try it. You may fall, but eventually you will learn how to ride it. The same is true for any skill.

With intellectual activities, you learn from a master who explains the basic theory and demonstrates how to solve problems. Once you understand what to do you are ready to try it. And it is only through repeatedly solving problems that you learn. Isn't this the way you learned mathematics? Only after you have done multiplication could you say that you know how to multiply. Only after you have solved a few square root problems could you say you are proficient in square-root solving.

You learn by doing. You learn how to write by writing, how to listen by listening, how to speak by speaking, how to solve puzzles by solving puzzles.

You learn through practice, practice, practice!

How did Itzhak Perlman become one of the greatest violinists? By spending 4 - 5 hours each day practicing. How did Zig Ziglar become a top notch professional speaker? By a long career of speaking. How did Dustin Hoffman become a great movie star? Hours of practice.

According to an old Chinese proverb,

> I hear and I forget. I see and I remember. I do and I understand.

You will understand better if you experiment. Experimentation can sometimes produce unexpected and thunderous results.

On May 16, 1954, Roger Gilbert Bannister, his arms and legs throbbing with unendurable pain, collapsed almost unconscious after running a mile in a fraction of a second less than four minutes. The entire world applauded. He became a hero, not only to sport followers, but to millions of ordinary people.

Bannister's feat had been considered to be impossible for thousands of years. Yet he was able to do it. Why? Determination, of course. And fourteen years of practice. He entered a race when he was eleven and finished in the eighteenth place. He didn't like that so he worked at it and began winning races. He went to Oxford University where he ran and won more races and steadily decreased his running time.

But determination and practice are not the entire answer. He experimented intelligently. hile Bannister attended Saint Mary's Hospital Medical School in London to prepare for a medical career, he developed an experimental approach to the improvement of his runnning. He ran on a treadmill and measured the oxygen he consumed. He then calculated the amount of oxygen he needed to consume in order to beat the four-minute mile. After many such experiments conducted over several years, he concluded that he needed to run the entire race at the lowest possible average speed. After practicing according to his findings, he was able to break the four-minute-mile record.

Bannister was acclaimed by the world for his *physical* feat. But it was his MENTAL feat, his ingenious experimentation which made his physical feat possible.

And what is experimentation but an extension of dialogue? After you do something, you ask yourself questions about the results. Are the results good? Are they what you expected? What do you think caused variations? Is there another, better way, to accomplish the same thing?

Experimentation is one of the most powerful approaches to learning. And, as Ralph Waldo Emerson said, learning is the essence of life:

> All life is an experiment. The more experiments you
> make the better.

E—EVALUATE AND CONCLUDE

Whether you get your information from published studies or from your own observation and experimentation, you must evaluate it.

Studies are in the news every day. As a result of a study done by prominent professors, sugar is bad for you. Tomorrow, another study by other professors says sugar is good for you. Coffee is bad for the heart. No, it is not bad at all. Only the caffeine is bad. Not really—decaffeinated is worse than the original coffee. No—only certain types. The latest is that we are not sure.

Studies are being produced about everything. Should you pay attention to these studies. Definitely. But evaluate them. Ask question, such as:

WHO PAID FOR THE STUDY?—Be skeptical of a study on smoking financed by the Tobacco Institute. Or of a study on Republican actions financed by the National Democratic Committee. Or a study on air pollution financed by the auto industry.

WHO DID THE STUDY?—Was it done by people of integrity following rigorous scientific procedures? Was it done by someone who does not have an emotional or financial stake in the outcome?

HOW WAS THE STUDY PERFORMED?—Was the study rigorous and scientific? If you are not sure, check with someone who is more familiar with the area of inventigation.

ARE CONCLUSIONS WARRANTED LOGICALLY? - Maybe the conclusions are too broad. Perhaps they apply only in certain cases. Perhaps the results are inconclusive.

With reference to polls, there are at least two more questions to ask:

WHAT KIND OF SAMPLE WAS USED?—Was the sample representative of the population being studied? Was its nature determined statistically? Was it of the proper size? Or was it the result of viewers calling into a talk-show host? Or constituents writing to their representatives?

WHAT TYPE OF QUESTIONS WERE ASKED?—Some questions are ambiguous. Some are leading questions. Some are suggestive of things which are not said. A slight change in a question can produce completely different results. Suppose I asked you, "Do you want to pay taxes?" No doubt you will answer "No". But if I asked, "Would you like to pay taxes in order to secure our country against foreign attack?" You are more likely to say "yes".

A—AMEND AND TRY AGAIN

After reaching a conclusion, you amend your mental framework according to what you have learned. If your conclusion is satisfactory to you, follow it with action. Nothing is accomplished without action. Now that you have learned something, use it. This is the so-called follow-through which distinguishes the mere dreamer from the performer.

If the results of your thinking process are inconclusive, ambiguous or not what you expected or wanted, repeat the process.

Now that you are a little smarter, you know better questions to ask. Repeat the I-D-E-A loop. Repeat the loop as often as necessary until what you learn is useable. Then act.

Following the I-D-E-A loop is not as easy as it sounds. Too many of us learn a lot when young. We try different approaches and finally settle on one best way. This is our script and we use it everytime. For true learners the I-D-E-A loop is endless. Results are used to form new hypotheses, which in turn lead to more questions, which initiate another turn of the loop.

LEARNING NUGGETS

Learning consists of seeking knowledge through mental activity, rather than through the gathering of information from external sources.

- **DON'T BE AN INFORMATION SPONGE—don't allow yourself to be inundated with what other people consider important**

- **I—INQUIRE AND DIALOGUE—find information important to YOU by questioning, listening, and searching**

- **D—DO AND EXPERIMENT—develop your knowledge through thorough involvement**

- **E—EVALUATE AND CONCLUDE—rigorously follow the rules of logic to arrive at a useful conclusion**

- **A—AMEND AND TRY AGAIN—repeat the I-D-E-A loop until you decide on a course of action and then act.**

Chapter 9

Take Risks For Creativity

Eureka! Eure-e-ka! Eure-e-e-ka!

Archimedes ran through the old Greek city of Syracuse naked exclaiming with exhilirating joy, "Eureka (I found it)."

What did he find? Archimedes found the solution to the problem given him by the king of Syracuse. The king had recently obtained a crown and he was suspicious of its composition. He asked Archimedes to determine whether the crown was made of pure gold or not.

Archimedes performed an experiment to test his hypothesis: Two objects of the same weight and made of the same substance should displace the same volume of water. He weighed the crown, placed it in water and measured the volume of water it displaced. He then took pure gold of the same weight as the crown, placed it in water and measured the volume of water it displaced. The two water-volume displacements were not the same. He proved that the crown was not made of pure gold.

This was a very rational procedure, based on logic and objective observation. But rationality and objectivity were not what caused Archimedes to run excitedly through the streets naked. It was intuition which stirred him so.

Some time after he had been given the problem by the king, Archimedes stepped into his bathtub and noticed he displaced a certain amount of water. From this simple observation—which is seen and unappreciated by almost everyone—he perceived the answer to his problem. All the knowledge he had about water, weights, volumes, and matter combined in his mind in such a way as to tell him the hypothesis he needed to test. What joy!

What insight! What intuition! What creativity! What exhiliration!

Did the creativity of Archimedes depend on his powers of intuition? His use of logic? Definitely. But his creativity depended more on his mental attitude.

The *creative attitude* is one of controlled passion, where you are eager to take a risk and stretch your mind to pursue a problem important to you. It helps a great deal if you are confident and relaxed. Specifically, to be creative:

- **Break Your Habits of Thought**
- **Stretch Your Imagination**
- **Evaluate Your Intuitions**
- **Embroider Your Rationality**

BREAK YOUR HABITS OF THOUGHT

Naturally you want a mind that is creative. A mind that conjures new ideas, concepts, and ways of doing things. A mind that produces innovations. A mind that can come up with unusual solutions to old problems. The trouble is your mind—as well as everyone else's—is often blocked. You have learned how to solve certain problems, and often you assume a new problem is similar enough to one of these problems that you apply the same solution. You overlook the differences. Such thinking is crippling to creativity. To be creative, you need to take a risk and leave the well-worn paths.

Script-Based Thinking is Crippled Thinking

The story is told about a group of space researchers who were trying to design a writing device that would work in space. The problem was that because the force of gravity is infinitesimal in outer space, the ink would not flow. After working on this problem for several months, the scientists gave up and asked a retired Nobel Prize winner for help. He came up with the solution almost immediately: a *pencil*!

Although the people in this story were space researchers accustomed to hard thinking, they nevertheless traversed the same old routes they had become accustomed to. They could not think in a different way. They developed a mental block.

Roger Schank says that as we grow up we learn formulas, specific ways of doing things, normal reactions to different situations. He calls these learned techniques *scripts*. We have scripts for shopping, entertaining, working, socializing—everything. Using scripts in our thinking is fine as long as we keep improving our scripts. The trouble is that after awhile, we come to depend upon our scripts without thinking about whether they truly apply in current situations. Schank calls this stuck-in-the-mud thinking *script-based thinking. Not creative!*

Creative Thinking is Risky Thinking

According to Schank, creative thinking is the direct opposite of script-based thinking. To be creative, always keep improving your scripts. Don't assume the same conditions apply as before. Ask questions and probe for differences. Don't be afraid of failure. Expect it. I quote him:

> The single most important element in learning is failure, and since creativity is an outgrowth of learning, failure is also important for creativity.

When we follow a script, we expect certain results. When they do not materialize, we have what Schank calls an *expectation failure*. Creative people seize upon such failures to learn. They question why, offer explanations, try to remember a previous analogous experience, question relationships between the two, and produce a generalization. This is a new expectation. If again they have expectation failure, they repeat their investigations over and over and over again until they reach their expectations.

He feels that creativity is not a gift bestowed upon a special few, but an attitude which can be adopted by anyone. Yes, being creative is more a question of attitude than talent or ability or brain power or intuition or perseverance. You need to be able to tolerate failure, even welcome it. You need to be willing to take a thousand failures for the opportunity of one successful creation. Elbert Hubbard said:

> The greatest mistake a man can make is to be afraid of making one.

The poet John Keats tells us:

> Failure is, in a sense, the highway to success, inas-
> much as every discovery of what is false leads us to
> seek earnestly after what is true, and every fresh
> experience points out some form of error which we
> shall afterward carefully avoid.

Creative people take chances.

They experiment. Try something new. Rearrange things.
Generalize. Specificy. Elaborate. Visualize. Change viewpoints.
Introduce randomness.

Highly creative people take BIG chances.

I especially like Schank's example of a highly creative person:
Vinod Khosla. Khosla is the founder of Sun Microsystems, a
successful manufacturer of advanced computer workstations.
The company developed a network file system which allows two
different types of computers to share data. What is the established
script for marketing such a device? You patent it. You make
yourself the exclusive source for it. You license it to others for
as high a fee as you can get. Khosla did none of these. He put
the device into the public domain. Data General, Digital Equipment Corporation and a host of other competitors used it and the
Sun approach became the benchmark in the industry!

Always be ready to abandon your most cherished scripts.

STRETCH YOUR IMAGINATION

The most profound learning comes from the unfettered mean-
derings of the mind as it follows its imagination unrestrained by
fear of failure. It is an exploration. It is an adventure into the
unknown. It is a self-directed pursuit of understanding.

DeBono, an authority on creativity who is quoted by everyone, calls this imaginative approach *lateral thinking*, to distinguish it from *vertical thinking*, a term he uses for script-based
thinking. Lateral thinking, non-script-based thinking, imagination—whatever it is called, it is a powerful way to use the mind.
It occurs in brainstorming, an important part of almost every
current quality-improvement program. Experimenting may be
another form of lateral thinking. The experiments of Roger

Bannister, which enabled him to beat the four-minute mile, demonstrate its creative power.

Sidney Parnes, a professor of creative studies, says:

> Creativity is a function of knowledge, imagination, and evaluation. The greater our knowledge, the more ideas, patterns, or combinations we can achieve.

Let your imagination stretch and roam and open new vistas. A good rule to follow is:

Try Something Different.

You need to constantly ask, "What if....?" If I changed a factor, what would happen? If I changed a relationship, what affect would it have? Suppose I revised my viewpoint, reversed my perspective, changed the order of things, tried to see things from another person's point of view, performed a different experiment. How would the picture change? Try different things and observe what happens.

Dr. Edward Jenner, the great scientist, was searching for the cure for smallpox. He thought that cowpox and human smallpox were related. Instead of asking himself why people get smallpox, he turned the question around and asked why dairy maids, who worked around cows, did NOT get smallpox. His investigation led to the conclusion that injection of cowpox gives protection against smallpox. He discovered one of the great vaccines.

A change in question led to a change in viewpoint, which led to a more fruitful mode of thinking. How do you know what questions to ask? Your previous experience will suggest questions. But often you don't know. You take a stab. According to the AI scientist Herbert Simon

> Human problem solving, from the most blundering to the most insightful, involves nothing more than varying mixtures of trial and error and selectivity.

Use your imagination in choosing a trial, and if your choice is in error, try again. All you need do is keep imagining and trying and eventually you will find the solution.

EVALUATE YOUR INTUITIONS

As wild and irrational as you may get when you unloose your imagination in your search for novel ideas, those that please you must eventually be tested. This sounds reasonable enough. Yet it is resisted by many who believe their intuitions are infallible guides to action. Intuition must always be checked by rational means.

The Four Phases of Creativity

Poincaré subdivided the creative process into four phases:

PREPARATION—The first phase consists of total immersion in the solution of a problem.Previous related work is evaluated, data are gathered, hypotheses are formulated, experiments are performed, discussions are done, logical inferences are drawn, and mathematical techniques are applied.

INCUBATION—If no solution is found, or if the solution found does not appear to be the best possible, you put your work aside. You do something else. Relax your mind. What you are really doing is giving the problem to your subconscious mind.

ILLUMINATION—After a period of incubation, it suddenly may come to you as a flash, an inspiration, an intuition. This may happen anywhere, while you are doing anything. Friedrich von Kekule was at home dozing at his fireside when he "saw" a snake biting its tail. Thus he solved his problem: he depicted the molecular structure of benzene as a ring.

VERIFICATION—After your flash of intuition, you must verify it. Does it solve the problem? Does it fit all the constraints of the given circumstances? Is it practical?

Rationality Supports Intuition

After all, what is intuition? Nobody seems to be able to define intuition in a manner satisfactory to all of us. I will not attempt to do it here. But it is well known that "it"—however you define "it— usually occurs to a person who is very experienced at what she is doing, after she has single-mindedly investigated and ostensibly considered all aspects of a problem. She is thoroughly committed to the task.

What does this imply? The implication, as expressed by the four phases of creativity, is that to produce intuitions that can be applied to practical purposes, you need to:

PREPARE FOR INTUITION—You prepare rationally. You search for facts. You investigate and study what other people have done. You propose hypotheses and do objective experiments. You draw conclusions in a logical manner.

VERIFY YOUR INTUITION

EMBROIDER YOUR RATIONALITY

I place a lot of emphasis on rationality: being objective, following the rules of logic and experimenting to unearth new information or to gain better understanding. But, just as intuition must be verified, so must rationality be occasionally embroidered - if you want to be creative. There are times when a little dose of subjectivity and more emphasis on non-logical forms of reasoning may hurl you into the creative mode.

Modifying your rationality helps in problem solving as well as in art.

Problem Solving

One of the pillars of scientific investigation is the development of theories to explain the known facts. How is this done? Rarely through rational means. It takes imagination, intuition, and visualization. The history of science is replete with stories about the power of imagination, but I like best the one about Albert Einstein. Einstein asked questions about light, such as:

> What would happen if a man should try to imprison a
> ray of light?

Not only did he ask such questions, he imagined himself at the end of a ray of light and visualized what would happen to him as he traveled through space under the posed conditions. In effect, he was imagining the way an experiment would work out. Then, relying on his intuition, he was able to come up with his

Theory of Relativity. Nothing rational about this. A very subjective approach. But what results!

Embroider your rationality with a little subjectivity. Try speculating about possibilities, instead of always relying on facts. You almost never have all the important facts anyway. One technique for solving problems in business and industry is brainstorming. In this approach you forget rationality and practical constraints. You open your mind and allow whatever ideas you have to pour out. The results of brainstorming sessions are often exhiliratingly surprising.

A few powerful non-rational methods of reasoning are:

INDUCTION—Although we speak of inductive *logic*, induction is not always done in a rational way. Induction is a process of finding patterns in data. Induction is what you do when you develop a theory, form a hypothesis, or see a problem, not in terms of its components, but as a whole.

ANALOGY—You say that one thing is similar to another, and draw conclusions from this. *Analogy* is used by good teachers to explain complicated principles or ideas. Earlier in this book I drew an analogy between your vision of your life and a movie: both are dynamic and not static.

METAPHOR—Unlike an analogy, which relates things with similar characteristics, the *metaphor* is applied to something in order to suggest a resemblance. An example of a metaphor is desktop publishing. Instead of thinking of shuttling marked-up manuscripts back and forth among writer, editor and printing houses, one may now think of doing all the writing, editing, illustrations, design and printing while sitting at a desk.

Art

Art requires preparation, experimentation and insight. Both rational and non-rational thinking are needed.

John Constable, the English painter, said:

> Painting is a science, and should be pursued as an inquiry into the laws of nature. Why, then, may not a landscape be considered a branch of natural philosophy, of which pictures are but experiments?

Tchaikovsky, the great composer, said:

> Generally speaking, the germ of a future composition comes suddenly and unexpectedly. If the soil is ready—that is to say if the disposition for work is there—it takes root with extraordinary force and rapidity, shoots up through the earth, puts forth branches, leaves and finally blossoms.

Creativity does not depend on how smart you are or how intuitive you are. Creativity is an attitude of experimentation, of trying many outlandish things, and of taking a risk.

LEARNING NUGGETS

If you want to be creative, intellectually or artistically:

- **BREAK YOUR HABITS OF THOUGHT—and open your mind to fresh ideas**

- **STRETCH YOUR IMAGINATION—keep trying something different until you find the gem that glows**

- **EVALUATE YOUR INTUITIONS—verify or modify your ideas to make them practical**

- **EMBROIDER YOUR RATIONALITY—do intuitive leaps of thinking to expand your horizon.**

Chapter 10

Direct Your Own Learning

Learning does not depend upon the educational establishment, the business establishment, or the political establishment. It depends upon you. No one else.

There are huge differences between education and learning:

*   Lecturing is *education*. It makes the teacher feel good. But it is not learning. LEARNING occurs through dialogue and discussion.

*   Dispensing facts, events and theories is *education*. It is easy for the teacher. But it is not learning. LEARNING occurs through thinking, imagining and problem solving.

*   Maintaining a highly structured and orderly environment is *education*. It too is easy for the teacher. But it is not learning. LEARNING occurs through the exercise of personal initiative.

*   Getting students to regurgitate facts to the teacher is *education*. It makes the teacher happy. But it is not learning. LEARNING is a creative activity and depends upon personal risk taking.

*   Trying to motivate students to learn is *education*. It pleases professors of education. But it is not learning. LEARNING depends upon self-motivation.

*   Maintaining an authoritarian environment is *education*. It is loved by education administrators. But it is not learning. LEARNING flourishes in an open democratic environment.

* Making schooling mandatory is *education*. It keeps education unions strong. But it is not learning. LEARNING
  thrives best under voluntary conditions.

* Testing for national standards is *education*. It boosts the
  importance of the educational establishment. But it is not
  learning. LEARNING depends upon personal standards.

* Labeling and giving credentials to students is *education*.
  It pleases business leaders. But it is not learning.
  LEARNING occurs every day in the mind of the individ-
  ual.

* Setting classroom policy is *education*. It helps members
  of the school board feel they are doing something important. But it is not learning. LEARNING happens through
  personal involvement.

Learning is a personal matter. Only YOU should direct your
own learning. Not a teacher. Not a professor. Not a corporate
trainer. Specifically:

- **Don't Submit to Educators**
- **Design Your Own Learning Program**
- **Choose Your Own Learning Collaborators**
- **Choose Your Own Learning Experiences**

DON'T SUBMIT TO EDUCATORS

A huge educational establishment exists ostensibly to help
you. And it can. But not if you put yourself entirely in its hands.
Like all establishments, the educational establishment's primary
concern is to keep itself alive and strong. Your concern is with
your personal intellectual health and mental growth.

You do need the educational system.Unfortunately, the
schools like to pour information into your head but do not make
you think problems through. However, with the proper attitude,
you can benefit greatly from the school system.

The proper attitude is a questioning one. As you proceed in
your schooling, you question more and more the guidance you
are receiving from your teachers. You begin to pick and choose
your subjects of study and your teachers. By the time you arrive

in college you should rely less on external guidance and more on your own inclinations. During your working life, all your learning should be directed by you. ou need to learn about:

YOU—The most important subject in the world for you to understand is YOU. What are you like? What feelings move you? What skills do you enjoy? What do you crave to do? What are you truly good at? How do you relate to others? What do you think is important? As the Greeks said, "Know thyself."

YOUR INTELLECTUAL DOMAINS—Your vision requires you to be knowledgeable in certain areas. You know what they are. Spend a lifetime studying, doing problems, and honing your skills in these domains.

YOUR ENVIRONMENT—You are not alone. You are part of a community of people in your field. Learn as much as possible about this community as well as other communities which impinge on your activities.

Don't allow educators or other experts to choose your learning goals, to modify your intellectual journey, or to change or distort your vision. This is not their function and as the unusual educator John Holt says:

> You can not have human liberty, and the sense of all persons' uniqueness, dignity, and worth on which it must rest, if you give to some people the right to tell other people what they must learn or know, or the right to say officially and "objectively" that some people are more able and worthy than others.

DESIGN YOUR OWN LEARNING PROGRAM

Since you choose your vision you should be the designer of a learning program to reach your vision. You know what you need to know. Your learning does not depend primarily upon teachers, but upon the activities and experiences you indulge in and the people you interact with in your day-to-day life. Your learning design should be about:

DEVELOPING SKILLS—There are many mental skills you need to develop to smooth the path to your vision. Most of these skills require some instruction. But for the most part, you can develop these skills by exercises and through use. Choose your skills and define your approaches.

USING LEARNING TOOLS—New learning tools, from books to sophisticated software, are being made available daily. With these tools you can learn by yourself theory or practice. Keep yourself informed about new learning tools. They could have a profound effect upon your learning design.

ACCESSING EXPERTS—There are many things you can learn by yourself. But not everything. Bou need experts: teachers, trainers, or knowledgeable people with gifted explanation capability. The important thing to remember is that YOU should choose the experts. From the point of view of your learning, the school or university is of secondary importance to that of the person who does the teaching.

CHOOSING EMPLOYERS OR BUSINESSES—Instead of seeking employment that pays the most, choose employers who offer a chance to learn and develop. Not training, but learning.You will enjoy it more and eventually make more money. Similar remarks apply for choosing a business to get into.

JOINING ASSOCIATIONS—Every professional group, every trade group, and every business group has an association where common issues, developments, and problems are discussed. They disseminate new technical information. More learning takes place in the conventions run by some of these associations than in elite universities.

CONTRIBUTING TO COMMUNITIES—You are a member of local, economic, social, political, and global communities. By contributing to one or more of these communities, you can learn a lot. It may not be obvious on the surface, but such work will help you reach your vision.

CHOOSE YOUR OWN LEARNING COLLABORATORS

You learn best from others through a collaborative and essentially egalitarian process. For the most part, we think of learning as being done in schools, universities, and training organizations by teachers and trainers. Although most of them are prescriptive and authoritarian, there are a few teachers and trainers who have adopted the collaborative approach.

Teachers, Who Are Learning Facilitators

Carl Rogers, the eminent educator, said:

> Teaching, in my estimation, is a vastly overrated function.

What then is the purpose of education according to Rogers?

> I see the facilitation of learning as the aim of education.

A *facilitator* is one who sets the stage for learning. She does not indulge in role playing. She is herself—a person. She allows her students to be themselves. She is one who understands how to let loose the curiosity of students. She nourishes their sense of wonder. She provides resources and tools for the students to use as they see fit.She encourages them to constantly ask questions. She gets her students so excited about learning, they initiate learning projects and activities on their own.

A facilitator is a *catalyst*. In chemistry a catalyst is something that is there to aid a chemical process. In education, a catalyst is there to aid the learning process. The learning takes place in the student's mind.

The teacher, the learning catalyst, builds an environment conducive to learning.

An excellent example of a learning catalyst, is Peggy Allan. Peggy Allan is a teacher at Greenville Junior High School in Greenville, Illinois. In 1988 she was the Illinois Teacher of the Year.

She believes in rippling. At the start of a semester, she asks each of her students to bring a rock that reflects his personality. Then she asks them to imagine tossing the rock into a great pond to produce ripples. One instance of rippling occurs when they learn a new word. They share the word with their parents who sign a "ripple card".

Rippling is one way Allan sets the stage for learning. Another way is by encouraging students to use their initiative. And initiative is stamped all over the research project the class did on nuclear power. Shortly after the Chernobyl nuclear disaster in the Soviet Union, the students discussed this issue. Since Greenville is a short distance from a nuclear power plant being built in Clinton, they wondered if a nuclear disaster could happen in their town. They decided to learn as much as they could about nuclear energy.

Peggy got things started by getting an Illinois Power Company official to address the class. This resulted in more discussion and in the decision of the class to divide into groups, each researching a different aspect of nuclear power. The students went to newspapers, magazines and to the nearby college library. They wrote to the Nuclear Regulatory Commission and the American Nuclear Society. They telephoned local experts.

Here are a few things the students accomplished:

*   A public survey of nuclear knowledge and opinion

*   Drawings of a nuclear reactor

*   Cost overrun study of the nearby Clinton Nuclear power plant

*   A study of radiation

*   A study of the five major ways to produce electricity

*   Hosted a seminar on nuclear power!

The seminar was a huge success and a source of pride to the parents and to the entire community. Experts were invited. The students made their presentations. People in the community asked questions. The highlight for Peggy Allan came when a member of the audience asked a question of the power company official. He did not know the answer, but one of the students did!

From this project, Allan's students learned mathematics, science, writing, drama, communications. More important, they learned how to think and solve problems by themselves.

Peggy Allan is a great teacher because she does not teach. She does not set herself up as the authority, an approach which may have worked in the Industrial Society. But not today.

Trainers, Who Act as Coaches

Good training encourages the trainee to perform in his own way. A good trainer demonstrates and then allows trainees to perform. He demonstrates again and then allows trainees to perform. Trainees learn by doing, comparing what they did with what was demonstrated and trying to get closer and closer to the demonstrated ideal.

A master trainer who I believe foreshadows what training soon will be like in THE LEARNING SOCIETY, is Rou De Gravelles. Located in Newport Beach, California, he helps people learn the art of public speaking, an art that will need to be mastered in the future by more people than ever before. I have had the privilege of being trained by Rou. No, he did not train me. He helped me learn. I never knew the difference between being trained and learning until I met Rou.

You must be a learner—I can't use the word student—under his guidance to truly appreciate what he does. But I will try to give you an idea. Basically he demonstrates speech delivery techniques and then has you speak. Your speech is recorded on video. You watch your video performance and then you speak again. That's the entire strategy. But what a way Rou has of implementing this strategy!

To begin with, he knows how to make people feel at ease on the platform. I have watched people rise with sweaty palms, palpitating heart, shaking knees, queasy stomach, a cold sweat over their bodies, and speak haltingly in a monotone. Rou makes a suggestion or two and these same people are speaking excitedly about their work or hobbies. The transformation is so great, everyone in the audience applauds. The new speakers are so exuberant about what they accomplished, they can't wait to try again.

Rou never teaches. He never tells you what to do. He never criticizes. He never compares you with anyone else. He never evaluates you. He never gives tests. He makes a suggestion, demonstrates what he means and asks you to try it. His favorite way of phrasing a suggestion is:

> You are very good at what you are doing. But try
> something different. I'm not saying that it is better.
> It's just another way. If it feels right for you, use it. If
> it doesn't feel right, don't use it. YOU make the
> decision.

Of course, his demonstration is so effective and what he says
sounds so reasonable, you try it. Almost invariably, you find the
new approach better. This increases your trust in him.

Rou believes that you learn by doing. He's there only to help
you practice the right things. I have never heard any teacher or
trainer, except Rou, say:

> The way you learn to speak is by speaking. If you must
> choose between making a speech before a group and
> attending a speech training session—even mine—
> speak before a group.

CHOOSE YOUR OWN LEARNING EXPERIENCES

Most of what you gain from other people is information. To
convert this information into knowledge you need to have experiences. Not passive experiences, let-the-expert-do-the-work experiences, relax-and-it-will-come-to-you experiences. But
learning experiences.Active experiences. our-mind-thoroughly-
involved experiences.

I believe that the greater the degree of your involvement in
the activity the more intense the learning that takes place. Here
is a list of activities sequenced from the least to the greatest
involvement, and from the least to most intense learning:

WATCHING TELEVISION—This is the most passive activity. Most of it is meaningless to you in terms of your vision.
You are not involved. Your learning is close to nil. Even the
famous anchor of ABC's Nightline program, Ted Koppel, says,
"On television, in place of truth we have discovered "facts."
..............We now communicate with everyone and say absolutely
nothing. We have reconstructed the Tower of Babel and it is a
television antenna."

ATTENDING A LECTURE—Because you have made a
choice to attend, you are somewhat more involved than when

you have flipped a TV switch. You want to hear what is said. But if you are merely exposed to words, the amount you learn is limited.

READING A BOOK—Here too you make a choice when you pick a book. Furthermore, it is difficult to read a book without paying close attention. It is an absorbing task. The amount of learning that can take place is great. But it is mostly theoretical.

PARTICIPATING IN A DISCUSSION—Participating in a discussion can be—depending on the type of discussion, of course—more active and more rewarding than reading a book. The first is a two-way flow of information, whereas the second is a one-way flow.

INTERACTING WITH TRAINING DEVICE—Even though the training device is automated, if it gives you an opportunity to interact (converse) with it and to receive critique and suggestions, your involvement is at a higher level than the activities given above.

MODELING BEHAVIOR IN WORKSHOPS—Here there is no automation. Everything is live. The emphasis is not on theory but on practice. Someone demonstrates how to do something. You model her behavior as best you can. She suggests improvement. You try again. You are thoroughly absorbed in what you are doing. This is the highest degree of involvement you can experience in a training situation.

DOING AND EXPERIMENTING AT WORK—The most involvement and the most learning occurs when you do work, especially if it is the type of work you enjoy. If you have an experimental attitude toward your work, the amount of learning is greatest of all.

Choose your own learning experiences. Choose reading material with care. Choose learning situations—schools, seminars and workshops—where you experience the greatest involvement. Choose your working environment—business organizations and associations—which gives you an opportunity to be creative.

LEARNING NUGGETS

Getting an education is not the same as learning. Direct your own learning activities.

- **DON'T SUBMIT TO EDUCATORS—they may guide your intellectual health, but only you know what you need for intellectual growth**

- **DESIGN YOUR OWN LEARNING PROGRAM— since you know your vision better than anyone else, you are the one who can determine the skills, learning tools, experts, employers, associations and communities that should be part of your learning**

- **CHOOSE YOUR OWN LEARNING COLLABO- RATORS—more mutual learning takes place when teachers and trainers act as collaborators**

- **CHOOSE YOUR OWN LEARNING EXPERI- ENCES—active experiences in your areas of interest are the greatest learning experiences.**

Chapter 11

Make Learning A Lifetime Habit

The importance of learning has been recognized by men of intellect and achievement from both Greek and Hebrew times. Socrates epitomized the Greek love of learning. The Hebrews had a saying:

Learn as though you were going to live forever

Live as though you were going to die tomorrow

They believed that you should be learning every single day of your life. Constant learning makes each day more interesting, more enjoyable, and more fulfilling. In other words, make learning a habit. The learning habit enhances your vision and your life. As John Dryden said:

We first make our habits and then our habits make us.

As a baby you were born with the learning habit. You applied the I-D-E-A loop all the time. Did you—INQUIRE AND DIALOGUE? Sure. It seemed as though this was all you did. Your parents were tired out answering your why's. Did you D—DO AND EXPERIMENT? Of course. You handled everything you could lay your hands on, and tasted everything that looked interesting. Many a thing you broke because of your experimenting. Did you E—EVALUATE AND CONCLUDE? Your evaluations consisted mostly of perceptions about what you thought were good or bad. But you did evaluate and draw conclusions. Did you A—AMEND OR ACT according to your evaluations? You bet you did. If you burnt yourself touching a hot stove, you were more careful next time. If your mother punished you for misbehaving, you changed your behavior the next time. If you fell down riding a bicycle, you picked yourself up and tried again and again.

What became of your learning habit as you grew older? You learned how to take care of yourself. You learned certain skills. You learned about what is happening in the world about you. You learned your scripts. And now you use them. Have you substituted the habit of choosing scripts for the habit of learning?

If you find yourself taking things for granted—following scripts—stop. Everything changes. What you learned was true or good yesterday, is not necessarily true or good today. You need to always be learning. You need to constantly be on the lookout for ideas, techniques, explanations, solutions. Return to your childhood habit of learning.

Your learning habits are the windows to your world.

Use these windows. Keep opening new windows. Keep the windows clear. Learn how to see and make sense of what you see through these windows. Learn how to share your window sightings with other people.

Your attitude toward learning defines the kind and number of windows you have and use. You can regain and then further develop your learning windows, by strengthening one or two attitudes related to each of the items in the I-D-E-A loop. For I, it is inquisitiveness. For D, creativity. For E, judiciousness. For A, both perseverence and cooperativeness.

To become a glazier of the mind, you need to:

- **Be an Observer**
- **Cultivate Your Creativity**
- **Balance Analysis with Intuition**
- **Be a Person of Action**
- **Excel in Human Relations**

BE AN OBSERVER

Inquisitiveness—always looking out the window—is a natural state. It is probably the most important habit for you to develop for effective learning. *Inquisitiveness* is a combination of curiosity and skepticism.

Curiosity gets you to ask questions. You ask questions of yourself: Who am I? What do I desire? What do I like to do? You ask questions of another person: What are you like? What do you like to do? How can I help you? You ask questions and expect explanations of a book: What are you saying? Make clear what you mean. Give me an example. You ask questions of nature: Why, when, how and under what conditions does this happen?

Your mind is open and eagerly anticipates the answers. Nevertheless you are skeptical. You do not accept the answers you receive at face value. You ask more questions to assuage your skepticism. You try to uncover errors in observations. You ask how results were arrived at. You search for sources of bias or error. You check for fallacies in thinking. You keep asking until you feel confident of the answers you are receiving.

To be a good observer you need to know how to be:

LOOKING—When peering through the window, you know where to look, how to look and what to look for. You pick up all the details, even those which may be somewhat hidden. When you read a book, you are able to absorb the major points. When you search a library, you can quickly gain access to the book you need. When you are listening to a speaker, you hear her body language as well as what she says.

FILTERING—Although you pick up details, you know how to filter what you see so that only what you need is recorded in your brain. You see patterns. You pick out patterns you are interested in.

CULTIVATE YOUR CREATIVITY

Creativity is definitely an attitude. It is an attitude toward work: you work hard and then you relax completely. It is an attitude toward risk: you experiment with many "crazy" ideas. It is an attitude of self confidence. To be creative you need to be constantly:

TRYING NEW THINGS—Try different ways, follow diverse approaches, pursue unusual ideas, experiment with alternate hypotheses.

USING YOUR IMAGINATION—Don't stick to conventional approaches. Think in new ways. When forming a hypothesis, look beyond the the ordinary and hum drum. Use analogy and metaphor and let you imagination soar.

When you are creative you are always opening new windows, windows with different shapes, sizes, colors and degrees of amplification.

Creativity is within you as it is within all of us. All you need do is keep opening and changing windows and it will do wonders for your psyche.

BALANCE ANALYSIS WITH INTUITION

Evaluation requires judiciousness. Like creativity, judiciousness requires both rationality and intuition. Both are helped by a good memory. Judiciousness is not innate. It can be cultivated. Cultivation consists of cleaning and polishing your windows until they sparkle, until they show what's happening without prejudice, until they bring the intimate details and relationships of what's happening to your mind.

Developing Analytical Capability

Observations are the raw materials for your thinking and problem solving. If the entire picture coming through the window is too complex for you to think about at once, you want to be able to separate it into its component pictures. You want to do analysis.

When you *analyze,* you apply the rigorous rules of logic and mathematics to painstakingly look at myriads of details to determine that:

METHODS ARE APPROPRIATE—Check hypotheses, experimental method, and techniques used. Are there any hidden assumptions? Are certain constraints disregarded?

DEDUCTIONS ARE LOGICAL—See if deductions made anywhere in the I-D-E-A loop are logical. Do they violate any logical fallacies?

STATISTICAL CONCLUSIONS ARE CORRECT—Do this especially when evaluating polls and economic forecasts. Check for bias in sampling and in the questions asked. Check whether written conclusions are justified based on the developed average, median and other statistical numbers.

Incubating Your Intuition

Thinking occurs at both the conscious and unconscious levels. For want of a better term, thinking at the unconscious level is often called *intuition.*

I mentioned before the four-stage creative cycle: *PREPARATION, INCUBATION, ILLUMINATION* and *VERIFICATION. PREPARATION* and *VERIFICATION* are done by the conscious mind. *INCUBATION* and *ILLUMINATION*, the two stages related to intuition, are done by the unconscious mind. In other words, to reach *ILLUMINATION*, to arouse or incubate your intuition, requires a shift in your consciousness. You may say that intuition comes from somewhere deep inside you.

Incubating your intuition illuminates the window to your Self.

Creative people know how to tune into—incubate—their intuition. Here is how Jonas Salk, the discoverer of the polio vaccine, feels about his intuition:

> It is always with excitement that I wake up in the morning wondering what my intuition will toss up to me, like gifts from the sea. I work with it and rely on it. It's my partner.

Intuition can not be actively called. But you can produce conditions conducive to its arrival. All you need to have a succesfull *INCUBATION*, that is, one that leads to *ILLUMINATION*, is to prime yourself with background knowledge, and be confident and relaxed. When illumination comes, you must grab it or it may fade away.

A few incubation techniques are:

RELAXING THE BODY—Always after working hard at your task, take time off before trying again. If you are at it for a very long time and not reaching a useful conclusion, get into the habit of relaxing thoroughly. Relax your body with rest, physical exercise or play.

QUIETING THE MIND—After your body is relaxed, you eliminate mental fatigue and remove sources of mental stress. Then through breathing exercises, Yoga, or meditation, you still your mind.

INVITING INTUITION—One way is to make suggestions to your unconscious before going to sleep: this is the problem, see what you can do. This is not a structured process and does not call for high concentration. Philip Goldberg, author of a book on intuition, says, "If we issue an open invitation and make intuition feel that visits are welcomed at any time, it can become a perfect guest, showing up on all the right occasions, dressed properly and bearing felicitous gifts."

TRUSTING INTUITION—Intuition does not come readily to most of us because we do not trust it when it does come. You must trust your intuition more. Begin to rely on it and it will come more often.

Mastering Your Memory

A good memory may be achieved primarily through the development of associations. William James, the great psychologist, says:

> The secret of a good memory is ...... the secret of forming diverse and multiple associations with every fact we care to retain.

You may form associations through mnemonics (the I-D-E-A loop is an example); by using several senses, such as you may do at a seminar, where you listen, watch a demonstration, write notes, and do exercises; and by painting vivid pictures in your mind representing people you meet.

To make sure you retain an important piece of information, you may want to repeat it over and over. Periodically after you have learned something, repeat it or use it. If you don't do this, no matter how well the information was registered in your mind, it eventually becomes difficult to retrieve.

BE A PERSON OF ACTION

To amend and repeat the I-D-E-A loop often enough to produce reliable results and then make a decision and act upon it requires perseverence. If you procrastinate amending the loop, the value of your previous steps may be nullified. Perhaps you may repeat the loop after a long waiting period. This may extend the time for learning, and if conditions change rapidly - as is true in many cases today - you may never catch up. If you do repeat the loop often enough to make a good decision, and then postpone acting on it because of uncertainties, events may pass you buy. Finally if you do not act on your decision, nothing will happen. You will not learn because you will never be sure if your decision was good or bad.

I am reminded of the rivalry between Eckert-Mauchly Corporation and IBM. In the early days of computers, in the early 1950's, I was working for the Eckert-Mauchly Corporation, named after the inventors of the UNIVAC. Eckert was the supreme engineer and Mauchly was a brilliant mathematician—a brainy pair. They had an excellent product, far superior to what IBM came up with at that time. However, Eckert and Mauchly were never satisfied with the current product. They constantly found things to improve. They delayed introductions. IBM became their nemesis because IBM management's attitude was entirely different: if a product worked, they stopped development and sold it. The result? Eckert-Mauchly, later Remington-Rand, consistently produced the best product, while IBM just as consistently made the most sales.

Timing is of crucial importance when making decisions. To be a person of action you need to know how to determine the time for:

CONTINUING TO STUDY—If your results are inconclusive, unclear or you believe you are on the wrong track, repeat the loop. Don't wait. The longer you wait, the less likely you are to be able to make a good decision.

MAKING A DECISION—Don't wait until you have looked at all the data and considered all the alternatives. Don't wait until you're 100% positive of your decision. That day may never arrive. Most decisions, especially the important ones, leave you with doubts about their being the right ones. Make the decision.

ACTING—Making good decisions can not help you if you do not act on them. Without action, you are a dreamer, not a dreamer of visions, but of fantasies. Act and act boldly.

EXCEL IN HUMAN RELATIONS

Throughout this book I place great stress on high technology. High technology is transforming our society. High technology is restructuring our organizations. High technology is providing us with learning tools to enhance our learning. Nevertheless it is human relations that will help you most in pursuing your vision. It is human relations that will help you in each of the four steps in the I-D-E-A loop. It is human relations that is especially important in the action step.

As I have said before, and it bears repeating, you can accomplish almost nothing by yourself. A cooperative attitude is the key to practical learning and accomplishment. The more you help other people, the more other people will help you.

As a learner, you keep looking through your windows, while other learners are looking through their windows. You have your vantage point. They have a different vantage point. You help them see things as you do. They help you see things as they do.

Cooperation effectively increases the windows of your world.

As a cooperative person you spend a lot of time with people:

GAINING MUTUAL UNDERSTANDING—You have empathy. You get to understand the visions that drive and make other people do what they do. At the same time you let them know about your vision. Understanding of people's visions leads to understanding of people.

COMMUNICATING—The art of communication is the most important of all the skills you need to have, regardless of what kind of vision you have. You need to communicate your thoughts and ideas through speaking and writing. These are best improved with constant exercise and application.

I have a lot more to say about human relations in the last section of this book, which discusses leadership.

LEARNING NUGGETS

Make learning a natural part of your life by adopting the following habits:

- **BE AN OBSERVER—keep looking and searching for information that fuels your learning**

- **CULTIVATE YOUR CREATIVITY—always be ready to take a risk and use your imagination to try a novel idea**

- **BALANCE ANALYSIS WITH INTUITION—use both your rational and intuitive capabilities in support of each other**

- **BE A PERSON OF ACTION—persevere in your learning, don't delay your decision, and be ready to follow through with action**

- **EXCEL IN HUMAN RELATIONS—cooperate with others through empathy and good communication.**

SECTION III

LEARNING TOOLS

To Enhance Your Learning

Chapter 12

New Technologies Of The Mind

There is a fable told about the pencil. Long ago, before people could read and write, the Master lectured and his students memorized and recited. Over and over and over they did this until the students retained the information. In this environment a young student came to his Master and initiated the following dialogue:

Sir, I invented a pencil.

A *pencil*? What's a *pencil*?

By means of a *pencil*, you'll be able to lecture better and your students will learn better.

Is that so? If I ate it, would my lecturing improve? If my students ate it, would their memorization ability improve?

With my invention no memorization will be needed.

No memorization? How will my students learn?

They will write what you say.

What do you mean by *write*?

Write means putting your ideas down on paper.

I see. And how long will it take for my students to learn to write?

About a year.

And then I will teach the same way? What's the difference?

There will be a big difference. The slow learners will be able to read your notes.

Read? What's *read*?

Read means to retrieve the information written on the paper.

And how long will it take for my students to learn how to read?

About a year.

And *notes*? What's *notes*?

Notes are what you will write to help students remember the main points.

At this the Master became angry, and said:

Are you telling me that my students will have to take two or three years to learn to read and write. I will have to take as much time to learn to read and write and then maybe another year to write notes. And then after all this time, I will lecture the same way as I always have. You're crazy. It makes no sense. Forget it.

But Master, there are many other advantages..............

You can't prove any. Besides, haven't we always learned by memorizing?

As everybody knows, the pencil made it. The Sumerian pencil, at about 3,500 BC, was a sharpened stick applied to a clay tablet. The Egyptian pencil, around the same period, was a reed brush applied to papyrus. The Roman pencil was an iron stylus, with which they wrote on papyrus; the papyrus was folded into sheets and sewn together to become a "book". The Greek pencil was a hard hollow reed cut at one end to produce a tip shaped like a modern pen with a slit through the middle. The fifteenth century pencil was the printer, the invention of Johannes Guttenberg.

The Industrial Society pencil was the machine and the physical goodies and gadgets it produced; all this physical bounty was due to the work of the physical scientists. THE LEARNING SOCIETY pencil is the computer and the intellectual tools it is spewing out; this intellectual bounty is due to the work of mental scientists.

The computer is different from other devices in that it is "hardware" which accepts "software" to accomplish various tasks. The "hardware" may be compared to the brain and the "software" to the mind. These entities are discussed in the following sequence:

- **The Physical Brain**
- **The Intellectual Mind**
- **The Hardware "Brain"**
- **The Software "Mind"**

THE PHYSICAL BRAIN

In recent years scientists have discovered the basic structure of the brain. They have determined that the brain is divided into two hemispheres and that when we think information flows among many nerve cells called neurons.

The Two Hemispheres

Early in the twentieth century, the neurologist, Kurt Goldstein, had a patient with these bizarre symptoms: She would bring her left hand to her neck and try to strangle herself. With her right hand she would pull the left hand away and sit on it. Then she would cry out, "I can't control my left hand."

From these and similar events, scientists have determined that the brain consists of two hemispheres. If you make a fist with both your right and left hands and bring them together, this forms a rough representation of the left and right hemispheres of the brain. The left hemisphere is responsible for rational activities and speech. The right hemisphere is responsible for perception activities and physical actions. Connecting the two hemispheres and acting as an information bridge is the Corpus Collasum.

In the above patient the Corpus Collasum was damaged. One hemisphere could not communicate with the other hemisphere. In order for the left brain, which controls speech, to affect action it needs to communicate with the right brain, which it could not do in this case. All it could do is say that it had no control over the left hand.

Neuron Town Hall

Within each hemisphere there are billions of tiny neurons. Each neuron has many tinier wires called dendrites which pick up information from associated neurons, and an axon at the other end which sends information to other neurons. This makes for a huge network of criss-crossing information.

The neurons act together as in a town-hall meeting. Each neuron receives signals from other neurons. It then votes—sends a signal out to associated neurons—when the sum of the incoming signals exceeds a threshold based on experience. Thus each neuron's vote depends upon the votes of associated neurons as well as its own bias. This system enables the brain to recognize patterns, associate meanings with various patterns, and to control our hands, feet, and other body movements.

Suppose we see a clown and then buy a ticket to a circus. What goes on in the brain? Think of three layers of neurons. First, there is a sensory layer which picks up patterns of light—we see a man, a red nose, colorful clothing. Second, there is a representational layer which gives meaning to the patterns of the first layer—they are converted into patterns representing concepts such as circus, enjoyment, family, funny. Third, there is a motor layer, which translates meanings into actions—we go to the box office and buy a ticket.

THE INTELLECTUAL MIND

The computer was instrumental in getting scientists to understand that the conceptual mind is just as real as the physical brain. Furthermore, there appear to be at least two minds: a rational mind associated with the left hemisphere, and a perceptive mind associated with the right hemisphere.

The Mind is Real

For a long time psychologists were trying to make psychology a science like physics. B.F. Skinner, the noted behaviorist, advocated that scientists should not concern themselves with the mind

—with ideas, concepts, motivation. These are not physical objects. They can not be studied objectively. Scientists should study only what they can see, hear, feel, smell, and taste. Never mind what happens in the head. Study the world outside the head to find out what stimulates a person. Then study the reactions or responses of the individual. By studying stimuli and responses, scientists can determine the nature of human behavior.

But when some scientists began testing theories about the mind by simulating them in the computer, psychologists began transforming their views of the mind. Behaviorism began its descent.

Here is an inanimate machine playing around with ideas and concepts, manipulating symbols, performing intellectual feats, and coming up with reasonable and useful conclusions. The computer is real, though it produces nothing physical. The paper the reports are printed on is not the true output of the computer. The ideas on the paper are. The computer is real. The intellectual results it produces are real. Not only the brain, but the mind, which handles ideas, concepts, and symbols, must be real.

Once it was determined that the mind is real and can be studied, the next step was to seek to discover how the mind works.

The Rational Mind

The Greeks believed in a *rational mind* which works with symbols and follows rigorous rules of logic and works with syllogisms, such as

> All Americans are smart
>
> John is an American
>
> Therefore John is smart

This formalized approach, which is also fundamental to mathematics, depends entirely on symbols.

The Perceptive Mind

We humans find this formal symbolic thinking difficult because it is too far removed from every-day life. Most of us rely mainly on our *perceptive mind* which develops from our experience. Early man stepped into the jungle and immediately sensed danger. He didn't actually see the beast, but he perceived that he was there. The pattern of sight, sound, and smell was similar to patterns he was familiar with because of previous observations and experiences. He knew the beast was getting ready to pounce and this perception made him ready.

What a person perceives depends not so much upon current observations as upon previous experiences. Learning is the capturing of experiences and relating them to each other to form patterns. These patterns or stereotypes are used to interpret further observations.

Most people believe that perception depends upon memory. And it does, but not the way normally supposed. We do not store complete images of what we see. We store *prototypes*. Instead of storing a picture of a hotel with all its lobbies, rooms, ball-rooms, restaurants, swimming pools and shops, we store a few characteristics of a typical hotel such as a Hilton. This is a prototype. A martini is a prototype for a cocktail. A robin is a prototype for a bird. A Honda is a prototype for a car.

A prototype is a stereotype. It is a specific way each of us has of observing. We do not see the same way a camera sees. We use our built-up stereotypes as interpreters of the scene our eyes pick up. Each person witnessing the same event "sees" something different. Each person therefore "remembers" something different. I was talking to my cousin the other day about my sister's wedding which had occurred over 40 years ago. He remembered that it was outdoors. So did I. He remembered wash hanging from clotheslines nearby. I remembered no such thing. I remembered a beautiful sunny day, a green lawn and a pretty wedding canopy under which the ceremony was performed. I remembered that the canopy was pretty, but didn't have the faintest recollection of its shape or color.

Matching patterns—a stereotype is a pattern—is what the perceptive mind does. This is why the perceptive mind is good at problems of classification and categorization. This is why the perceptive mind can recognize a face at a glance.

The *perceptive mind* is subjective: it is based upon its previous experiences. The *rational mind*, however, follows an objective approach which is unrelated to its experiences. Which is better? We need to depend on both to be creative.

THE HARDWARE "BRAIN"

To correspond to the two hemispheres of the brain, there are two broad types of computer hardware: the rational computer and the perceptive computer.

The Rational Computer

The conventional digital computer is a rational machine: it is a vessel for holding and manipulating a program of symbolic instructions—*software*.

The first commercial computer, the UNIVAC, cost a million dollars; consisted of rows upon rows of cabinets containing big vacuum tubes; occupied a huge air-conditioned room with false floors under which cables ran; handled only the simplest types of programs which nevertheless took months, sometimes years for an elite crew of analysts and programmers to write; needed input from punched cards, magnetic tape or other difficult-to-use devices; required daily preventive maintenance operations; and produced primitive results.

From a monster machine used by elites the computer has become a portable appliance used by all people. It has become small, easy to use, inexpensive, and above all, extremely powerful. Now you may enter data via a keyboard, a mouse (a pointing device), your voice or a pen. Instead of learning a machine language, all you need know is English and perhaps remember a few commands. The price has come down from the millions to the hundreds. If the Cadillac had come down a proportional amount it would now cost 65 cents. At the same time computer power has zoomed.

Best of all, the computer has shrunk. Its shrinking is due to the computer technologists who have found ways to place more and more electronic components in smaller and smaller spaces. Today we have a *computer chip*, which stores hundreds, thousands, and even hundreds of millions of circuits on a piece of silicon, the size of a fingernail. Scientists and engineers are working on techniques to use tiny atoms and even DNA, the material all living things have that define their nature, to produce invisible chips containing BILLIONS of circuits.

The Perceptive Computer

In recent years, scientists and technologists have developed a different type of computer, one that mimics the neurons in the brain. It is called a *neural computer*, or a *neural network*. At the present time a neural network consists of a great number of small processing units organized into at least three layers, somewhat akin to the organization of human neurons in the brain. Because neural networks are so good at matching patterns, they may be used to recognize speech, smell, human faces, signatures, and languages. They are *perceptive computers*.

To learn more about the brain, scientists are planning to build a neuronal model of it. Since there are billions of neurons in the brain, building a model of it is an immense undertaking. However, scientists are busy preparing for this endeavor by mapping all areas of the brain. The scientist David Waltz says that by the year 2017 the neuronal chip will be so small and cheap that we will be able to build a neuronal model of the brain for about twenty million dollars.

THE SOFTWARE "MIND"

At the present time, it is software for the rational computer that is the intelligence which can be a boon to you in your learning. When you learn you build models in your mind. Software that enriches your modeling capability amplifies your learning. Software packages are available to produce basic models, concept models, and dynamic models.

Basic Modeling

Just as clay is a basic material for modeling a physical object, a symbol is a basic material for modeling a mental object. Among the basic symbols are:

NUMBERS—Simple arithmetic is often used to model our actions, such as, buying, selling, and investing. The accountant models a corporation with numbers on spreadsheets. Spreadsheet calculations may be done with lightning speed on the computer.

WORDS—When you write a report, you model with words. To make your task simpler, you may use a word processor.

PICTURES—An artist models with pictures. With the graphics software available today any person can learn to produce drawings and pictures just as easily as she may produce a written report.

MULTIMEDIA—You can now integrate numbers, words, and pictures in audio, video, and graphic media in the same system. The opportunities for modeling have increased tremendously.

Concept Modeling

A *concept* is a network of relationships. You may think of a hierarchy of concepts from the simplest to the most complex. In terms of the range of information, you may think of the:

DATA MODEL—With a data base management system you may build a data base—a *data model*—that represents a corporation's accounts, a sales prospecting domain, the structure of the literature in a specific research area, or any domain of activity. The data base helps solve associational problems.

KNOWLEDGE MODEL—At the other end of the concept hierarchy is the most highly aggregated information. This is as close to knowledge as you can get. One type of *knowledge model* is the expert system (a form of AI), which offers advice after conversing with you to determine the problem.

Dynamic Modeling

Basic models and concept models are models of static situations. *Dynamic modeling* includes the element of time. Among the many ways of doing dynamic modeling are:

TIME MANAGEMENT—Time-management packages offer calendars, yearly planners, project scheduling, and help you analyze where your time goes.

SIMULATION —Simulation is a way of effectively experiencing the future in accelerated time. It is an excellent way to design a complex system, such as a mass transportation system. First you define how you think the system would work. You determine the characteristics of major entities you need to be concerned about, such as trains, stations, passengers, traffic, and local merchants. You stipulate the frequency and conditions under which occur specific events, such as ticket purchasing, entering and leaving trains, and making purchases from nearby merchants. When you build a simulation reflecting all this and let it run for a given time period: five years, ten years or fifty years. In a fast computer, fifty years may take no more than an hour.

MANAGEMENT GAMES—Games are simulations which involve competition. In the business world, there are many management games, which enable you to "run" (simulate) a business and make moves to counter competition over a period of time. Games like these are risk-free methods for learning what to do in competitive situations.

The computer and the mental scientists who work with it have transformed our view of the world and brought us powerful learning tools. They are discussed in the following chapters of this section:

- **Design Your Global Learning Landscape**
- **Nourish Your Garden of Knowledge**
- **Enjoy the Fruits of Your Garden**
- **Apply Wisdom of Other Gardens.**

Chapter 13

Design Your Global Learning Landscape

This is the age of the individual. The age of learning. Whether you are in school or not, you are a student in the broadest sense of the word. You want to control your lifetime activity of learning. And today it is easy for you to do this, because high technology is there to assist you. With high technology you can design a landscape around your mental garden. This landscape begins in your home and can spread out to include other mental gardens—some of them automated—all around the Globe. It is a global network of mental gardens.

The first step in achieving your global learning landscape is to build your learning headquarters:

- **Design Your Learning Headquarters**
- **Acquire Tool-Building Tools**
- **Maintain Your Learning Headquarters**

DESIGN YOUR LEARNING HEADQUARTERS

Your learning headquarters should be a storehouse of tools for remembering, problem solving, and communicating with other people. The best receptacle for such learning tools is the computer.

Place one in your home office. You will have plenty of company. According to the futurist Marvin Cetron, by the year 2000 seven out of ten homes will have computers.

It's easy to use a computer. You don't need to know how to print books in order to read them. You don't need to be an automobile mechanic in order to drive a car. You don't need to be a computer engineer to design your own computer-oriented learning center.

The computer is the heart of your learning headquarters. It can store all the software learning tools you may need. With a modem, plus communication software, you can connect your computer to any other computer that can be reached with a telephone line.

If your computer is in a den or office of your home, this ostensibly makes your home your learning headquarters. Not necessarily. We now have laptop, palm-top, and purse computer "notebooks" and communication devices. With these, your learning center is wherever you are.

YOU are the central node of your learning network.

ACQUIRE TOOL-BUILDING TOOLS

The market is bulging with software products. Not all this software is useful for learning. Many are there to help you *avoid* learning. Just as physical products have been designed to save you physical effort, many software products are designed to save you mental effort. They have their place in streamlining your activities. But if you want to learn, you need to have tools that help you exercise your brain, not rest it.

The less strain on the brain, the less mental gain.

The least stress occurs when you use a tool which guides you step by step in a specific procedure. You have no idea what is happening. You do certain things and you get certain results. A perfect example is the cash register used by fast-food restaurants. The keys have pictures of different food items on the menu. The operator chooses the correct pictures and out comes the amount owed. No thinking. No learning. No advancement.

Completely on the other side of the spectrum is the *tool-building tool*. This is a piece of software which helps you build your own software tools. This approach is tougher on your brain. It forces you to think. It allows you to make changes. As a learner you are always making changes. This is why you need to concentrate on tool-building tools.

There are at least four kinds of tool-building tools:

* Storage and Retrieval

* Instruction
* Simulation
* Communication.

Storage and Retrieval

In the early days of computers it was found that for the computer to accomplish anything it needed first to find and transfer data; after the data was processed in some way, it needed to be re-stored so it could be easily found for another operation. In other words, storing and retrieving data is basic to the accomplishment of ALL tasks. This is true for machines and also for people. Thus began the development of storage and retrieval systems.

Many packages on the market today are essentially nothing more than storage and retrieval systems for specific applications, such as time management and sales prospecting. According to the instructions given, you store prospect names, company names, addresses, phone numbers and other pertinent data; then you may retrieve them following simple rules. These packages may also do simple calculations.

But very little learning takes place. For this you need a *data base management system*, a sophisticated outgrowth of the early storage and retrieval systems. The data base management system comes with a quasi-English language, with which a non-programmer can give it updating and retrieval instructions. A popular example is dBASE.

I call this a tool-building tool because with this system you can build a data model that expresses your needs. You organize and structure your data exactly as you wish. Naturally you do this to simplify your expected data searches. You want to be able to find what you need quickly.

dBASE, or any other data base management systems, is definitely tougher to use than a ready made piece of software. But it helps you learn. Experience with it helps you understand relationships among the data items in your data model. After awhile you may use the data base management system to modify your data model. You are learning.

Instruction

Another tool-building tool is the system which allows you to author an instructional package.

Early computer-assisted instruction systems consisted of thousands of individual frames and tests. Each frame contained a small lesson. Each test determined whether the student was ready for the next small lesson.It was an awkward system controlled entirely by the designer. It followed an authoritarian top-down approach.

Today we are beginning to see hardware and software with which any teacher can author a system which allows the student to control her learning. These systems use multi-media devices, such as CDs (compact disks), which can store the text in a 110-foot bookshelf, four to sixteen hours of music, or a complete one-hour color video show. The student chooses the next frame, which may be verbal, pictorial, audio, animation or a combination. The student is in charge of her learning.

Simulation

Twenty years ago, building simulations was a complicated affair. It required computer-knowhow of a high order. But today businesspeople do simulations all the time with electronic spreadsheets, such as Lotus 1-2-3.

The *electronic spreadsheet* duplicates an accountant's spreadsheet on the screen. One uses the spreadsheet the same way an accountant does his old fashioned spreadsheet, with one huge difference. Every time a person makes a change to the value in a specific cell - in a given column, at a certain row—she need do no more. All the numbers in all other cells which depend upon that value change instantly.

The numbers in the electronic spreadsheet represent the company's operations. By playing "what if" games, you could simulate operations over given time periods for different conditions. The electronic spreadsheet may also be used to build a numerical simulation of another activity—the economy, for instance.

Communication

To be a good communicator you need tools. Not ready made tools; you will be communicating someone else's thoughts. You need the ability to design your own communication tools.

A *word processor*, for instance. No, a word processor is not a sophisticated typewriter. With a word processor it is easy to change words, sentences, paragraphs; and if it has graphics capability, illustrations. Instantly you may bring a phrase from one location to another. Just as quickly, you may delete words, add punctuation, reverse order, interchange sentences. You may play with the text, try new versions of a sentence, reorder paragraphs. You may experiment with your prose to improve your communication.

The word processor is a tool for building tools for communication. This communication may be with yourself, as well as with others. A properly written report may help you organize your thoughts and remember them for later use. They also help you experiment with ideas.

How much more experimentation can you perform with a desk-top publishing unit! In addition to making it easier to rearrange text and to format the page for clarity, you can add diagrams, charts, illustrations and pictures as well as typographical design flourishes to make the message more inviting.

Experimentation is also easily done with presentation software. Here you can prepare a colorful slide show, which can be viewed directly on your computer screen. Or the slides can be converted into film or other media for projection.

MAINTAIN YOUR LEARNING HEADQUARTERS

Build your learning headquarters one strand at a time. Build and learn. Build it so that you have the best tools available for learning directly and from other people and systems in your network.

To do this you need to constantly track developments in the science of the mind, the technology of computers and communication, and the information services offered by people and organizations. There are developments on the horizon which may radically alter your learning and thinking patterns.

The new science of the mind is just getting started. The scientist Howard Gardner has developed a theory that there are at least seven types of intelligence. As a result of research in artificial intelligence, you may in the future converse with machines in English. Furthermore, you will not be merely a user, but a partner. You will no longer speak of a machine being user-friendly, but *conversation-friendly.*

The major trend in computer technology is toward miniaturization. This gives cause for rejoicing as well as for apprehension. Smaller and cheaper computers will spread their use and increase the learning level of the population. However, miniaturization tends to bring with it specialization. Special computers will be built for thousands of different tasks. It sounds good, but it isn't. With specialized devices, the devices do the task. You do nothing. Specialized devices rob you of your learning.

In communication, big changes are happening, especially in multimedia. Combinations of text, pictures, sound, video and animation are being perfected to produce startling realism. So startling that the technique is called *virtual reality.* With virtual reality, you can enter the scene and become part of the event. You experience the scene with your senses as though you are actually there!

The telephone line itself will become intelligent. When speaking to foreigners on the telephone, your words will be translated instantly: you will speak in English; your buddy at the other end of the telephone lion will hear it in French, Spanish, or Chinese.

Vice president Albert Gore has proposed the creation of a National Research and Education Network (NREN). He conceives this as an "information infrastructure" or a "highway for the mind", a superspeed communication network. On NREN it will be possible for medical centers to exchange all the 3-D X-rays and CAT scans on about 100 cancer patients in one second, or for weather researchers to access 1000 high-resolution satellite photographs in one second. Privately-run "highways for the mind" are also being proposed.

Today computers communicate with each other primarily by telephone. They may in the future communicate by radio waves. Maybe TV. Maybe computers and TV will be combined.

With all the expected discoveries in the science of the mind and the probable innovations in high technology, will come the proliferation of presently unheard-of information services. New information searching aids. New value-added-to-information services. New..........who knows?

LEARNING NUGGETS

To design your global learning landscape:

- **DESIGN YOUR LEARNING HEADQUARTERS— around a personal computer equipped with communication capability**

- **ACQUIRE TOOL-BUILDING TOOLS—building your own storage and retrieval, instruction, simulation and communication tools stretches your learning**

- **MAINTAIN YOUR LEARNING HEADQUARTERS—keep track of developments in mind science, high technology and people services to keep your learning headquarters up-to-date.**

Chapter 14

Nourish Your Garden Of Knowledge

In the center of your global learning landscape is your mental garden.

Your *mental garden* consists of trees, shrubs and other small plants growing in a design of your making. The trees are your life's work. You may be growing only one, a big tree, if you are absorbed in one field of endeavor to the exclusion of all others. Or you may be growing more than one if you have, like most people, several major domains you like to pursue. The shrubs and small plants are decorative additions, things you like to dabble in for profit or amusement. They give wholeness, character and beauty to your garden.

Your mental garden is both similar to and different from a home garden. Both must be meticulously designed for health and beauty (intellectual exhiliration). Both must be nurtured. Both must be cultivated. However, there is a great deal more unity to your mental garden than to a home garden. In a home garden each plant is more or less on its own. As a matter of fact, each competes with the others for sun, water and nutrients. In your mental garden all the trees, shrubs, small plants and everything else work together, cooperate in producing practical fruit and beautiful flowers. A fruit may not come off a particular tree without the help of other garden elements.

This unity shows another way. When learning a new subject, you start growing a new tree—until you discover many associations between the baby tree and an old established tree. The baby tree disappears and is reincarnated as several branches in the established tree. A stronger, healthier tree.

Your mental garden needs the warmth and energy of the sun, something it can get from the books and other learning tools in your home library. It also needs water, vitamins and minerals. In this day of technology, you can pipe the food in from other elements or nodes in your Global landscape. From automated mental gardens in your Global landscape, it may obtain specialized information with which to cultivate—solve problems in - your mental garden.

To nourish your garden of knowledge:

- **Illuminate It With Your Library**
- **Pipe In New Information**
- **Cultivate It With Specialized Information**

ILLUMINATE IT WITH YOUR LIBRARY

Your mental garden can't thrive without getting its primary life force from the sun—a steady radiation of facts, ideas, opinions, techniques, happenings, principles, beliefs, theories, myths, and fantasies.

Your library may contain printed literature, primarily books, but also magazines, workbooks, reference works, audio and video tapes, CDs, and pictures. Notes are another source. Whether from books, seminars or personal experiences, if saved, they can add significantly to your store of basic energy for mental growth. By including your computer, you can make your personal library a more powerful mental sun.

Book Reading

I read in the newspaper that 60% of the population did not buy even one book during the past year. People seem to get most of their information from watching TV. What a shame. Books are a thousand times better for illuminating your mental garden. There are many reasons. You choose the book you read. If you can't afford the price of the book, you may check the book out of the library for free. If you find it boring, you lay it aside. If you like certain parts, you dwell on them. If you don't care about other parts, you skip them. If you do not understand any section of the book, you review it. If you want to remember certain statements or injunctions or well-expressed observations, you highlight them with pencil or magic marker; for library books, you take notes. If you want to refresh your memory, you read the book again.

In the comfort of your favorite chair, in your favorite room, at your favorite time, you may curl yourself up with a book. You may stay with it for as long or as short a time as you like. When you are tired of it, you may put it down and pick it up at another time. YOU, not some character on the boob tube, are in charge of your mental stimulation.

Note Taking

Perhaps you have an outstanding memory. If you do, great. But if you are like me, you may read a book today and in a year or so forget its major thesis or a few of the pillars supporting the thesis. What to do?

Take notes. Record the major points so that when you are done you have a summary of what the book means to you. Record eloquent prose which you may quote, formulas which may be helpful in your problem-solving, procedures and examples that give the thesis life. File the notes away in file folders or in loose-life notebooks. They then become part of your library.

Why not do a similar thing when you attend a seminar? Often you come home from a seminar with a workbook, all scribbled over. The day after the seminar—don't wait, or you will forget important points—fix up your workbook so that it summarizes what you learned. If you need to add notes, this is the time to do it. Make a neat package and make it part of your library.

Don't forget the ideas that come to you at all hours of the day, unbeckoned flashes of insight, imaginative approaches to pain-in-the-neck problems, delightful intuitive realizations. Or the blinding ideas that strike you during the night. You awaken from dreams with pregnant thoughts you are convinced are good and right. Write them down or they vanish back into the subconscious from which they come. Add them to your library.

Using Your Computer

You may store books, magazines and loose-leaf notebooks in bookcases; file folders in file cabinets; and audio cassettes, CDs, video cassettes, file cards, and many other media in special containers. How do you organize all this information so that you may find the information you need when you need it?

The computer is the answer.

I do not mean to imply that all your information should be converted into computer form. Definitely not. This approach is good only for data that is dynamic, that is, data that is frequently entered, modified, or retrieved. Rolodex data. Sales prospect data. Inventory data.

I mean that a storage and retrieval system in your computer can be used to store an index of all the information packages in your library external to the computer. Let me use what I do as an example of what is possible. When I find a magazine article I want to save, I tear the pages out and staple them together. I also take notes of books I read. I file these information items in loose-leaf notebooks, classified by subject matter. Each item is labeled with a sequenced code number. For instance, if the item is about business, I give it a code number such as B101 and place it in the B loose-leaf book after the item labeled B100.

In the computer, I use dBASE to define a record for each information item stored in the loose leaf books. The record stores data about date, author, title, subject, source, a few other things which may be helpful for retrieval, and of course, the code number. When I search according to one or more of these characteristics, the computer supplies the code number—B101 in this example—with which I retrieve the article in my loose-leaf book on business, B.

The storage and retrieval system can also be used to print out a list of all the information items you have in your library, or all the items in certain categories.

PIPE IN NEW INFORMATION

In addition to the radiant energy you receive from your sun, your personal library, your knowledge garden needs food: news, about current events and about developments in your fields of interest. A newspaper is an excellent way to get the news. Like a book, you can read it where, when, and how you want. Also like a book, you can pick what you read and read as much or as little as you wish.

A more efficient way to keep informed on current events is to subscribe to an information source. Take, for example, CompuServe. CompuServe has what they call Executive News Service: you select the topics that interest you and they scan the wires and put together your personal newspaper. No longer do you need to be disturbed by stories that are of no interest to you. No longer must you leaf through page after page of advertising. No longer is it necessary to search stock, bond or other tables.

Let's say you want to receive political, financial, business, scientific and technological developments, as well as changes in individual stocks you own. Everyday you will receive a newspaper with only these features. A newspaper tailored to your requirements. When your requirements change, you may redesign your newspaper.

In a similar manner you can keep informed about the latest development in your field, whether it be medicine, law, education, science, art, music, government, social science, manufacturing, retailing—practically anything.

CULTIVATE IT WITH SPECIALIZED INFORMATION

In addition to water, vitamins, minerals, and other nutrients, a garden must be tended. The soil must be aerated, the weeds pulled, and the pests destroyed. Otherwise your living matter may become sick, produce sour fruit, or die. The problems are many and varied. You need help in the solution of these problems.

You need help in cultivating your mental garden too. This help often comes in the form of specialized information you may not be aware of. This specialized information is stored in over 5000 on-line data bases.A data base can be found about any subject you can think of. And many that never crossed your mind. They have been developed by corporations, universities, government agencies, think tanks, publications, and others.

With your computer, you may access a data base through specialized information utilities. They help you choose an appropriate data base and also help you in the search. To give you an idea of what is possible, here is just a tiny sample of tasks you may accomplish by searching scholarly and technical data bases via specialized information utilities, such as BRS, Mead Data Central, ORBIT, DIALOG and Dow Jones News Retrieval

SEARCHING FOR LEGAL PRECEDENTS—By accessing the LEXIS data base, a vast law library for attorneys.

FINDING BIBLIOGRAPHY ON SUPERIOR SCHOOLS
—By accessing BRS, which supplies data bases offering bibliographic references, not only on education resources, but on academic, business, financial, medical, and scientific research.

DOING CRIMINAL DETECTIVE WORK—By accessing NEXIS, a comprehensive news data base for journalists researching stories. When a man attempted to assissinate Pope John Paul II, a search of NEXIS uncovered the fact that Mehmet Ali Agca, an escaped murderer, had written a letter in 1979 threatening to kill the Pope when he was in Turkey.

RESEARCHING INVENTION PATENTABILITY—By searching the International Patent Documentation file, which contains bibliographic and family data for patent documents of 55 patent-issuing organizations all over the world.

UPDATING CANCER RESEARCH DEVELOPMENTS
—By searching MEDLINE, a data base covering all aspects of experimental as well as clinical medicine. It also stores information on dentistry, pharmacology, veterinary medicine, nursing, and biochemistry.

INVESTIGATING INVESTMENT OPPORTUNITIES
—By referring to Standard and Poor's Value Line and Disclosure data bases, which present detailed financial ownership data.

LEARNING NUGGETS

To nourish you garden of knowledge:

- **ILLUMINATE IT WITH YOUR LIBRARY—a compendium of books, notes, and other media organized for easy retrieval with the aid of your computer**

- **PIPE IN NEW INFORMATION—your personal newspaper tailored to your requirements**

- **CULTIVATE IT WITH SPECIALIZED INFORMATION—search any of 5000 on-line data bases to find answers to your problems.**

Chapter 15

Enjoy The Fruits Of Your Garden

Here you are, a mental garden in the center of a global learning landscape. Through direct activities in your home and through activities from information sources in your network you are nourishing your garden. This nourishment is constant. Without it nothing intellectually noteworthy can occur. However, if you have been feeding your garden a steady diet of high-level nutrients, you are in a position to reap its fruits and enjoy its flowers. The fruits of intellectual problem solving. The flowers of aesthetic exhiliration.

For most of your learning activities, you may depend upon software tools that you build. You have the tool-building tools. You can do this. If you have difficulty with technology, get someone to help you. It is worthwhile. You are learning.

There are situations where you would want a ready-made software product. Many of these specialized packages help you avoid mental drudgery in routine tasks. But beware. Too many of them are nothing but software gadgets, gimmicks and gewgaws. Those that appear to be useful, do all the thinking for you. They keep you mentally lazy.

Avoid these learning robbers.

There are, however, ready-made packages which are powerful learning tools. They are easy to recognize. Though they appear to be applicable to a specialized area, they nevertheless are generalized. By this I mean that they give the user flexibility. They allow him to take the initiative. They keep him involved and interested. They do not teach, but facilitate learning.

This chapter is concerned with learning you can do yourself with the aid of such problem-solving tools. Only a few possibilities are discussed. In this chapter I try to give you a flavor of what you can accomplish. Once in the groove of learning-tool possibilities, your imagination can take over and see how tools may be applied to your specific learning agenda. The next chapter discusses the learning you may achieve through your communication network.

With self-learning tools you may:

- **Learn New Domains**
- **Enhance Mental Performance**
- **Acquire a Skill**
- **Study a System**
- **Stretch Your Imagination**

LEARN NEW DOMAINS

When you are on the other side of the coin, you are the student and not the instructor, you want a system where you can learn through involvement. A few examples:

MAMMALS: A MULTIMEDIA ENCYCLOPEDIA—National Geographic transferred its *"Book of Mammals"* from print to CD-ROM. But it's a lot more than a book. The system enables a child to choose any of two hundred animals to learn about. She can hear the name of the animal properly pronounced, and even the way the animal howls or growls. By pressing a button, she can read about the animal's vital statistics and other pertinent data about the animal. She can press another button and see a picture of the animal's habitat. She can learn as much or as little as she wants about each animal.

WHERE IN THE WORLD IS CARMEN SANDIEGO? —In this game the student pursues master thieves who have stolen the torch from the Statue of Liberty. As she chases them from one city to another, the student gets to learn about these cities. Some people call this geography. But it truly is fun.

LOGO—Professor Symour Papert, of Harvard University, has developed what he calls a learning environment, a medium that allows children to learn by themselves. LOGO has a mechanical "turtle" which can trace a path on the screen in any direction. A child enters primitive commands to make the "turtle" trace vertical and horizontal lines. Without instruction, the child plays in this environment and in the process learns concepts about programming and about geometry. Children love to play and learn with LOGO. According to Papert:

> Education should be more like Nintendo than like books.

THE MAGIC FLUTE—The Audio Notes edition of Mozart's *"The Magic Flute"* is produced by Warner New Media. According to your choice you may see the libretto in English or German. Not only can you hear the opera and see the score, you can find out many different things about Mozart and the opera. You may get a musical commentary and analysis, hear a narration or the story, obtain an analysis of characters in the opera, and much more. Again, while enjoying the opera, you may learn as much or as little as you wish. You are in charge.

ENHANCE MENTAL PERFORMANCE

One of the best ways to enhance your mental performance is with an *expert system*—an automated consultant. An expert system can get you to operate at a higher mental level than you could ever do before. When you have a problem it advises you what to do.With time you learn how to perform without its advice. Two examples:

TAXCUT—This is a program for your personal computer which takes you step-by-step through the process of preparing your U.S. Income Tax Form. All the know-how of tax advisor Dan Caine is embedded in this software.

SAM (STATISTICAL ANALYSIS MENTOR)—It is designed for a novice statistical analyst. Since there are hundreds of statistical techniques to choose from, the beginner is often confused. SAM asks a few questions to determine the nature of the problem, and then suggests an appropriate statistical technique. It even explains its choices to help the user understand.

ACQUIRE A SKILL

Environmental simulators enable you to acquire a physical skill. I give two examples:

FLYING SIMULATOR—Here graphics are skillfully used to reproduce, not only the environment, but the way you interact with it. With the Flying Simulator you may try any flying maneuver in the safety of your living room or den. On the screen of the computer you see an airplane, whose movements you can control. You try a takeoff and the airplane moves across the screen according to your instructions. You point it in a given direction, give it a certain speed and the location of the airplane referenced to a ground map can be ascertained. You do a landing and the airplane lands. You learn how to fly under non-hazardous conditions.

TREE-CUTTING SIMULATOR—Weyerhauser Company hired Mark Lembersky, a former professor at Oregon State University, to design a simulator to show lumberjacks how to cut trees. Now you may say that having a professor teach lumberjacks their trade is ridiculous. But loggers were cutting trees inefficiently. Lembersky's simulator showed a chain saw and trees on the screen. With the aid of a joystick (a computer graphic input device) the logger could roll trees and cut the trees with the graphic chain saw. The logger made decisions on how to do the cutting and then the computer would show him the results of his decisions. The computer also showed the logger how his decisions affected company profits. The logger learned to modify his own behavior to improve the bottom line of the company.

STUDY A SYSTEM

Games are excellent tools for learning about systems. I give two examples: one a board game, the other a computer game.

MARKET SHARE—This board game is similar to some computer games. The purpose of the game is to learn strategic thinking. The board of 100 squares is subdivided into seven areas of the information industry: television, cable, radio, newspapers, books, magazines, and software. Five teams of two to three members each, compete. At the start of the game each team has roughly equal market share. Each team decides where to place its chips to increase its market share and to challenge its opponents. At the end, the team with the greatest market share wins.

SIMCITY—With this game city planners may simulate a city and its operations. The player, or learner, creates a city. He decides where to place police stations, energy plants, airports, parks; where the roads and train tracks should be; and how to zone, assess taxes and distribute revenue. On the screen of the computer the user sees the results of his decisions. He sees cars running on the highway and if not enough funds were given to the transportation department he sees bridges collapse. If a section of the city is too far from a fire station, the user sees small fires grow into big ones. Every action of the user brings a series of events. If he does not like the results he modifies his decisions.

STRETCH YOUR IMAGINATION

A great imagination is a priceless asset. It boosts, expands, enlivens your creativity. Anything that stimulates your imagination should be highly valued. Some software tools do this. Imagination stimulators are available to help you grow both your intellectual and artistic creativity.

MAXTHINK—This was invented by Neil Larson, a disciple of Dr. DeBono, the creativity expert. *MaxThink* has been called an idea processor because it helps you in all kinds of creative and writing projects. The basic idea behind it is that it allows you to manipulate lists. With it, you may organize your thoughts to develop a new idea from its embryo, to explore relationships among ideas, and to produce an outline for a book.

AUTOCAD—This software enables you to produce thoroughly detailed engineering drawings in three dimensions, even if you have never done drafting before. In an instant, you can make changes: moving lines or objects; modifying sizes or shapes. Such software has also been used to produce beautiful quilts.

COREL DRAW— This is only one of many graphics tools on the market. With any of these packages, you do not need to

mess with brushes and paints. You do not even need to be able
to draw a staight line. The computer can give you lines, circles,
squares and ellipses; a pallette of thousands of colors; instant
control of shading, shadowing, perspective, and symmetry. With
the touch of a key you can adjust the thickness of a line; vary the
size, color, shading, and light intensity of an object; and dynami-
cally move an object to a new location, rotate it, magnify it, do
airbrushing. You can do all sorts of experiments on a 3-D picture:
adjust symmetry by moving objects around, vary lighting to
change the viewpoint, repeat elements for emphasis, blend one
image into another, delete an object without any need to over-
paint, and erase everything and start again from a basic picture
previously stored.

When it comes to art most people are skeptical of the computer's utility. They believe that technology is far removed from
art. Rather than being foreign to the the artist, the computer may
turn out to be the best medium an artist ever had. It may even
make artists of non-artists. Though he claims he is not an artist,
Melvin L. Prueitt wrote a book about computer art. The book is
filled with his artwork, all good, all executed on a computer.
Here is what Prueitt writes in his book:

> Some critics have claimed that computer art cannot
> be true art since it is made by a machine. But a
> computer cannot create art by itself any more than a
> paint brush can produce a Mona Lisa. Computer art,
> like all art, is a product of the human mind, conceived
> through studious reverie. It does not depend on the
> manual dexterity of the artist but on the artist's ability
> to conceive new visual ideas and to develop logical
> methods for forming images (or to use the methods
> developed by others). In this sense, computer art may
> be closer to the human mind and heart than other
> forms of art. That is, it is an art created by the mind
> rather than the body.

Creative headway, though not as great as for fine art, has been
made in music and the performing arts. Music synthesizers as
well as tools for composing music have been developed.

LEARNING NUGGETS

Though tool-building tools are the best grounding for your learning center, there are specialized software packages which can help you:

- **LEARN NEW DOMAINS—because they encourage initiative and involvement**

- **ENHANCE MENTAL PERFORMANCE—by advising you in the solution of specific problems that enable you to work at your highest level**

- **ACQUIRE A SKILL—through the manipulation of an environment representing the real-life environment**

- **STUDY A SYSTEM—by artificially experiencing the events comprising the system**

- **STRETCH YOUR IMAGINATION—intellectually by suggesting associations; artistically by expanding your choices.**

Chapter 16

Apply Wisdom Of Other Gardens

Telephone systems cover the entire Globe with a lacy network. Any person can speak to any other person who has a telephone anywhere on the face of the Globe. All of us in the world are part of one verbal landscape.

But the landscape is more beautiful than this. Not only can people separated by thousands of miles converse, so can computers. People with their computers. People with their learning tools. Mental gardens with their intellectual gardening tools.

You are the center of your global learning landscape.

You with your learning tools. An intellectually-powerful combination. Made even more powerful by the intellectual synergy created when communicating with other people: colleagues, coaches, guides, catalysts, collaborators and specialists. Combined with their learning tools!

You learn from them. They learn from you. You learn together. To apply the wisdom of other mental gardens:

- **Communicate with Colleagues**

- **Network with Community Members**

- **Consult with Infopreneurs**

COMMUNICATE WITH COLLEAGUES

Whether you are an employee within a corporation seeking files from another location, a self-employed individual searching for technological data, or a researcher trying to work with a distant collaborator, you want your computer to communicate with other computers. A few methods used are:

LAN—A *LAN* (local area network) may be set up for people-and-computers communication within an organization, a group of cooperating organizations, or even among cooperating individuals. Almost all big corporations and many small ones connect different parts of their operations with LANs.

INTERNET—For university educators, scientific researchers, military analysts, and defense-industry professionals there has for a long time been a special high-speed communication network, call ARPAnet. ARPAnet was originally created by the U.S. Department of Defense. It is now known as Internet and it is run by the National Science Foundation. This network, which has been used primarily for communication among defense workers and their high-powered computers, is now used by universities, business organizations and individuals. It is expected to be the foundation for the "information superhighway".

BULLETIN BOARDS—A bulletin board (BBS) does what the name implies. On the board you may post notices and exchange information with people separated from you by distance but united with you in a community of interest. Whenever you wish you can communicate with one or all members of the community. There are tens of thousands of bulletin boards (BBS) run by user groups, associations, publications, universities, information utilities, companies, and individuals. Most are free.

ELECTRONIC MAIL—In ordinary mail, you write a letter, which is picked up by a mail-delivery clerk, brought to a post office, forwarded to another post office, and then delivered by another mail-delivery clerk. A time-consuming process. In *electronic mail*, you send an electronic message directly to a central location for fast receiver delivery. MCI offers electronic mail service with same-day delivery. If the addressee does not have a computer, he may receive a hard copy of the letter via the Postal Service the next day.

GENERAL INFORMATION UTILITY—You may join a *general information utility*, such as CompuServe, Prodigy, or the Source. These utilities offer BBSs and electronic mail, plus many other informational aids. In addition to their normal services, they may arrange access to specialized information utilities and their data bases.

NETWORK WITH COMMUNITY MEMBERS

Subscribers to an information utility may network with other subscribers. Here you may find members of your work community—the industry, the vocation, the market. Your learning community—experts, colleagues, students. Your learning-tool community—the hardware, the software, the procedure. Also your leisure communities.

CompuServe, for instance, has what it calls Forums, over 150 groups pursuing their specialized interests. Forums are available for people active in the same vocation or hobby, interested in the same subject or craft, or who enjoy the same entertainment or recreational activity.

Among the many networking possibilities are the following:

SCHMOOZING—Anytime you feel like taking a break from your normal routine, you may talk to your Forum friends. When you return to your work, you are refreshed. Often serendipity happens during your conversation. Either you or your converser may be hit with an inspiration.

ELICITING SOFT INFORMATION—A favorite way of using a Forum is to put a question onto the message board of your Forum. This may be something that has been bothering you. Or it may be an information-research question you need to have answered before continuing with your work. You have no idea how to get the answer from the library. So you post the question. Because of the nature of Forum membership, often a member will come up with the answer. She just happens to know the answer, because she just happens to have the relevant experience.

BOUNCING IDEAS—If you have a problem, you may pose a question on the message board. ou invite anyone who is interested to suggest solutions. Ideas fly. You may even start a brainstorming session. Before you know it you and your Forum buddies are bouncing several suggestions around. They are also helping you evaluate them.

LEARNING ABOUT LEARNING TOOLS—Every member of the information utility is using computers and has different software learning tools. If you have acquired a new piece of hardware or software and something about its use stumps you, post a question on the message board. You will be answered almost immediately. If your equipment is not working properly, post a question. Excellent advice from someone who has experienced the same problem will come back to you. If you want to learn about the latest learning tools available, post a question. Quick answers will be forthcoming. You may even receive direct to your computer new free software.

HOLDING CONFERENCES—Many Forums hold regularly scheduled meetings. Here you may discuss current hot topics. At some of these meetings, prominent people are interviewed. You may receive their files. Of course, you have the opportunity to ask them questions and participate in the discussion. If you like. If not, you can leave at any time.

COLLABORATING—Members of a Forum get to know each other pretty well. If you find someone who can complement you intellectually—he is strong where you are weak; you are strong where he is weak—you may want to work on a project together. It's easy to collaborate. You send your files to him. He sends his files to you. You may discuss the same message that you both see on your screens.

An example of someone who finds networking via information utilities excellent for getting ideas and accomplishing his work is Howard Rheingold, editor of *Whole Earth Review*. He says:

> Living on-line works for me as an editor; I know print
> editors all over the world who make networks work
> for them. Several of the best articles in *Whole Earth*

Review, in fact, began as informal exchanges on-line
with people I never met.

CONSULT WITH INFOPRENEURS

If you can't find the information you are looking for in an
on-line data base, nor through members of a BBS or information
utility, it's time to consult an information broker or infopreneur.

An infopreneurs is an on-line problem-solving librarian. For
a fee, she accepts a problem you may have, searches manual and
on-line data bases, travels to organizations and interviews people, and presents you with a report covering her findings.

An infopreneur is more than an efficient searcher. She solves
informational problems. If you need to learn quickly about a
newly-developing technology, such as biotechnology, she can
write a report that helps you do this. If you are planning a new
business, she can put together a potential-competitor intelligence
report. If you are doing a market survey, she can dig up a lot of
pertinent information.

So why worry about being informed? So many of us run
around like chickens with their heads cut off trying to be informed about everything. It can't be done. It shouldn't be done.
Today you have the luxury of being able to concentrate on growing
the knowledge you are interested in.

The infopreneurs of today represent only the very beginnings
of what I think will become one of the most important industries
of the future.

LEARNING NUGGETS

Apply the wisdom of mental gardens around the Globe:

- **COMMUNICATE WITH COLLEAGUES—get answers to your questions**

- **NETWORK WITH COMMUNITY MEMBERS—
  schmooze, get information, bounce ideas around,
  have a conference, learn about learning tools, and
  collaborate with talented people**

- **CONSULT WITH INFOPRENEURS—for tough informational problems call an information expert.**

SECTION IV

LEADERSHIP

To Enlist Others in Your Vision and Learning

Chapter 17

The Network Leader

Welcome to our newly-minted learning-tool factory. Our vision here is to help consultants give better advice with the aid of smart products.

For too long our economy has been absorbed with building physical products—gadgets of all kinds. Our cars have become bigger palaces. Our kitchens have turned into factories which are rarely used since eating out is so common. We seem to be shopping all the time. The major pastime, in addition to shopping, has become watching the boob tube, which innundates us with distracting, confusing, contradictory, and misleading information.

We've reached saturation in obtaining material things for our comfort. Why not concentrate on developing our intellectual, emotional, and spiritual natures? We know how to do it. We have the technology for building products to help us learn.

Our vision here is of an extremely flexible organization revolving around our employees and the visions and knowledge they possess. We believe in learning. We believe that the more our people know, the better will be our products and more successful will be the company. So we set up what we like to call learning communities. Everybody has teams nowadays. But not every team is a learning community.

By a *learning community* we mean one where any employee can approach any other employee and ask questions. This means that PhD's mingle with production people. This means that no one is in an ivory tower, no one here spends his time doing research and writing reports. This means that no one is better than anyone else. No one has the most important knowledge; some of the most crucial knowledge is possessed by production people. Everybody contributes to everyone's learning.

Our employees are expected to rap with the client. By that we mean, they should get to understand the client and what he is trying to accomplish so well that they can acticipate the client's needs. They are also expected to be adept at solving problems.

Our employees work in teams or as individuals, or in some other arrangement depending upon the circumstances. We have no separate department for training; training—a better word is learning—is the responsibility of everyone. We have no separate department for information systems; everyone is concerned with information, and more importantly, knowledge. We have no separate departments for organizational development, support, personnel, research and development, manufacturing control, quality control; responsibility for these functions is spread out to everyone.

Our vision here is to help each of our employees achieve his or her vision.

These are the words of a future entrepreneur as she speaks to a new recruit. As a true leader she knows that the center of society is no longer the huge organization or the entrepreneur, financier, or politician who can run such organizations. The center is the individual, who can paint and pursue a personal vision.

The center of our economy is no longer mass production of a physical product but the supplying of an intellectual product or service, something that can only be done by an individual, the source of intellectuality.

The center of vocational preparation is no longer the educational establishment, which was geared to supply the needs of the defunct Industrial Society. The center is the individual, because learning can only be accomplished by a person.

Organizations are restructuring so that they revolve around the individual. Instead of following orders from superiors and dishing out orders to inferiors, each individual interacts with other individuals in a flexible network arrangement. Each individual feels, or should feel, that he or she is the center of the network.

The change in the organization and its effect on leadership is given by the following progression:

- **Structure: Pyramid to Network**
- **Information: Up-and-Down to All Directions**
- **Culture: Management to Leadership**
- **Individual Leadership**

STRUCTURE: PYRAMID TO NETWORK

The old corporation had a rigid pyramidal structure. Over the years it has been changing to a more flexible structure, the network.

Rigid Pyramid

In the Industrial Society, once a capitalist invested in a factory, he became the BOSS and everyone else he employed was labor. As the factory became bigger, the BOSS hired several sub-BOSSES, and assigned each a separate sub-function. He gave them orders and they, in turn, gave orders to those below them. Eventually the BOSS constructed a functional pyramid: a hierarchy with himself at the apex, several layers of sub-BOSSES below him, and labor at the bottom. Labor did the work, the drudgery functions, and the sub-BOSSES reported what was happening up to the top. The BOSS then gave the commands, which were relayed down to the toiling labor below.

The two outstanding characteristics of the pyramid were:

RIGIDITY—The pyramid was divided into vertical levels and horizontal divisions. Each level required a different level of management. Each division was functionaly separate from other divisions.

HUGE SIZE The corporation was big. If new divisions were added horizontally more levels needed to be added vertically. From Albert Lee's book about General Motors, I learned that as late as the 1980's General Motors had fourteen—14— levels of management!

Flexible Network

Jessica Lipnack and Jeffrey Stamps, authors of a popular book on *networks*, define them this way:

> Networks are nodes linked together in order to do something, to achieve a purpose.

Nodes, links and purpose—these are the three key words. In an organizational network, the nodes are persons; everything revolves around the people. The links represent the various relationships among the nodes, the people; links are used to form groups, to relate groups to other groups and to relate one network to another. The purpose is whatever the network, the organization, has been set up to do.

Take a look at Brooktree, an advanced high-tech company which produces RAMDAC, a chip which is used in multi-media computer workstations. It has no factories of its own. It operates as a network and coordinates its activities with other companies around the world with the aid of a communication network. Its employees use sophisticated software at workstations, to design chips. They link their technology to the technology of various chip fabrication factories around the world via the communication network. Thus a device can be designed in the United States, fabricated in Japan, packaged in Korea and tested back in the United States.

Like the people represented by its nodes, an organizational network is a moving, changing, adapting, learning, living organism. As contrasted with the pyramid, the major characteristics of the network structure are:

FLEXIBILITY—Changes are easy to do and are frequently made to accommodate new realities as they occur.

SMALL SIZE—Perhaps there were economies of scale in mass production of the Industrial Society. But today, economies of scale rarely exist. Companies are shrinking. Even huge IBM, has recently subdivided itself into several smaller independent companies. The futurist Marvin Cetron states that by the year 2000, 85% of the workforce will be working for firms employing fewer than two hundred people. That the corporation will shrink further is supported by Tom Peters, the prominent business guru, who says, "I know that the future does not belong to the companies I grew up with, the elephants that used to rule the world and that I used to serve. These wild and wooly times call for a new species of competitor—fast, agile, thriving on change."

INFORMATION FLOW: UP-DOWN TO ALL DIRECTIONS

Information follows the structure of an organization. In the pyramid information flowed from the bottom up to the top man so he could make the major decisions. In the network information is used as a resource by all members and it flows in all directions and only when needed for individual learning.

Information System for Decision-Making

Each major corporation developed a management information system as a mirror image of the organization. Those on bottom wrungs did nothing but supply data to the system. Middle managers could access only information that they had "a need to know". Only the top executives had access to all the information. The system emphasized two major characteristics of the pyramid organization:

MANAGEMENT DECISION-MAKING—To make decision, those on top were supplied by their underlings with reams of reports, with rooms full of displays, and the results of computer studies developed by analysts, operations researchers, and others.

LEVELS OF MANAGEMENT—Top management made the big decisions. They allowed lower levels of management to make the less important decisions.

Information System as Resource

But information can not long be forced to flow in unnatural ways. People who need the information will find a way to get it. Furthermore, now we realize that more information does not necessarily lead to better decisions. For better decisions, knowledge is needed.

Knowledge is the product of an individual's mind. Every individual in the organization possess knowledge about her task. To improve her performance, she needs information. Thus the new concept of information as a resource—not to the organization, but to individuals within the organization.

Making information a resource for everyone leads to:

INDIVIDUAL LEARNING—To do her task better, each individual in the organization needs to learn. No boss, no teacher, no trainer knows better than she what information she needs in order to learn. She can access whatever information she needs.

REDUCED LEVELS OF MANAGEMENT—No longer does an employee need to go to a manager for information. As a result middle managers in the 1980s and early 1990s have been fired in droves.

CULTURE: MANAGEMENT TO LEADERSHIP

When the pyramid collapsed and the information system became a resource for individuals in the organization, the culture within the organization began changing. The idea of a manager as being superior and making decisions for everyone else began to be replaced with the leader who helps each person in the organization develop to his greatest potential.

The Authoritarian Manager

Management as a discipline was developed in order to run the big hierarchical corporation. The culture of the pyramid reflected its structure. It was:

AUTHORITARIAN—Whatever anyone does in the organization must be sanctioned by his boss. His boss, in turn, can not do anything that is not sanctioned by *his* boss. And so on. There is a chain of command. And woe is to him who breaks the chain of command.

CONTROLLING—Everything an employee did was under control of a supervisor or a manager. Status information was regularly gathered and evaluated about his activities. The results were used to further control the actions of the employee.

COMPETITIVE—Competition was endemic in the Industrial-Society organization. Employees on the bottom of the hierarchy hid things from those on top, just as those on top told the troops nothing about their plans. Each division competed with other divisions for money, materials, projects, and recognition.

The Democratic Leader

Leadership is becoming more important than management. We are not there yet. But the trend is in this direction. How does a leader differ from a manager?

> The relatively obsolete manager manages data. The new leader leads people.

This is the fundamental difference between the two, according to Joe Batten. And since the computer can manage data better than any human, what do we need managers for?

The implication of the old management culture was that there are superior people who could manage the affairs of other people. But Douglas Strain, chairman of Electro Scientific, doesn't like the artificial separation between management and other employees:

> The Harvard Business School view is too sterile. Their distinction between management and employee is far too sharp and not very productive. Lots of time management thinks that people have to be managed. But people manage their own lives before they come to work in the morning and after they go home.

He also says:

> Most management gets in the way.

The new leadership culture is based on the premise that each person in the organization is an autonomous intelligent human being capable of exercising initiative. To encourage self-development of each individual, the culture should be:

VISIONARY—A great company has a vision—usually an extension of the vision of its founder.

DEMOCRATIC—Up until recently, democracy in whatever form was considered anathema in the American corporation. But dynamic democracy is coming into its own, ironically, because of inanimate high technology. Free discussion, egalitarianism, teamwork, and voting are becoming more common in today's corporation.

COOPERATIVE—To increase cooperation among employees working on different disciplines but on the same product, companies have torn down the walls separating divisions and departments. The emphasis is on coordinating all activities related to a project or a product line.

It's tough to change the corporate culture from authoritarianism to democracy. But it was done by Ralph Stayer, the head of Johnsonville Sausage. Stayer spent ten years in his quest to take his company from the Industrial Society to THE LEARNING SOCIETY. As he tells the story, in 1980 he was running a herd of buffalo, but what he wanted was to lead a flock of geese.

A herd of buffalo follows a boss buffalo blindly. In the past, hunters were able to destroy a whole herd by targeting the boss buffalo. Once the boss buffalo was killed, the other buffalos did not know what to do. They were all slaughtered by the hunters.

Stayer realized that he was an autocratic boss. He made all the decisions: whom to hire, what to buy, what to sell. He began to realize that as a result, his employees were bored, marking time, following orders blindly, and making stupid mistakes such as mislabeling products. Since he was worried about new competition, he decided to change the company culture.

A flock of geese looked good to him. Geese fly together in a V-formation. They follow a leader. Yet each bird works essentially on its own. It took Stayer a long time to realize that to lead a flock of geese, he needed "geese" who would take responsibility for their own actions. He needed to allow people to express their power, the power they possessed because of their knowledge. Instead of a manager who controlled his people, he became a coach who made suggestions and communicated a broad vision. Instead of solving the problems brought to him by his managers, he returned them to the managers to solve. Instead of being responsible for the quality of the sausages, he gave the responsibility to those who made the sausages.

Stayer had been checking the quality of sausages by tasting them. When he realized that tasting gave him the responsibility, he asked the workers to do the tasting. Worker responsibility for quality led to many changes. Teams were formed. Teams began taking care of customer complaints, analyzing costs, evaluating labor performance, hiring and firing, scheduling work, and even approving capital expenditures. The six levels of management were reduced to three. Employees became known as *members*. Managers became *coordinators* and *coaches*.

The climax of the story came when a big but risky contract was offered the company. In the old days, Stayer says he would have conferred with his senior management team and probably would have turned the contract down as being too risky. This time Stayer allowed the members to make the decision. After a thorough discussion, they voted to accept the business. They worked hard to make the contract work. They succeeded magnificently!

Major milestones in the company transformation are made obvious by statements Ralph Stayer made as he progressed:

BEFORE TRANSFORMATION

I had made the company and I could fix it.

DURING TRANSFORMATION

From now on you're all responsible for making your own decisions [to his managers].

AFTER TRANSFORMATION

The end state we all now envision for Johnsonville is a company that never stops learning.

Notice the three new words: *we, envision* and *learning*.

INDIVIDUAL LEADERSHIP

In THE LEARNING SOCIETY leadership needs to be exercised by everyone. Even if you do not want to found a corporation. Even if you do not want to rise to be an executive in a big business. Even if you do not want to be a legislator, a governor or a president. Even if you want to work for someone else!

Individual leadership is expected even in the factory. Witness the leadership expressed by the amazing comments of production workers to a group of us attending a factory tour hosted by Beckman Instruments in September of 1989. The tour was part of a two-day Excellence Through Partnerships seminar. All the factory presentations were organized and presented by those who did the work. Here is a small sample of their comments:

> The four of us work here. We make sure quality is perfect. We do it all ourselves. Nobody else inspects our work.

> You'll have to forgive us. We are still trying to arrange this setup. It's not working the way we like it yet.

> I do all the spray painting. When I need paint I call the paint company myself. They deliver exactly the color I need and put it right on this spot. No red tape. No purchase orders.

So much for people who are employed. How about those who have lost their jobs? During the last twenty years Fortune 500 companies shed employees like each of us sheds garbage. Twenty years ago they employed 19% of the workforce. Today it is less than 10%. They have had mergers, acquisitions, hostile takeovers, and reorganizations. Many of those who are employed are temporaries, part-timers, or "independent contractors" who could be let go at a moment's notice.

All these people thought the corporation would take care of them.But no one can think like that today.Willy nilly, every person is challenged to provide a future for herself.

Everyone is an entrepreneur. Why be an unwilling entrepreneur when you can be a willing entrepreneur?

YOU must be an entrepreneur and you must exercise leadership. The way to exercise leadership is discussed in the following chapters:

- **Instill a Shared Vision**
- **Build a Learning Community**
- **Manage Learning Tools for Learning Community.**

Chapter 18

Instill A Shared Vision

$\mathbf{V}$ision is where everything begins. Vision is the most important element of future design and it is also the most important element in the leadership component of future design. Whatever you do is related to your vision. And when you form an organization or get an informal group to help you—when you are exercising leadership—the way to be effective is to get people to share your vision.

People who share your vision will follow you. They will be committed to what they are doing, perform admirably, and produce extraordinary results. To instill a shared vision among three people or three thousand people in your network:

- **Don't Be a Boss**
- **Communicate Your Vision**
- **Cooperate With Network Members**
- **Settle Issues Democratically**
- **Respect Each Person's Autonomy**

DON'T BE A BOSS

In the old Industrial Society the authoritarian manager followed a control model to assure himself that those reporting to him performed according to his requirements and expectations. Today in THE LEARNING SOCIETY the leader is guided by a mutual-development model.

The Control Model

The *control model* follows a feedback loop to assure stability. What is a *feedback loop*? First you set up a standard. Then you continuously check the status of whatever you are controlling against the standard. If the status deviates too far from the standard, you produce an action that brings the status back to standard. This last action is called *feedback*. To purpose of the whole loop is to keep everything within tight limits—under control.

The thermostat in your home uses a simple feedback loop to control the heat produced. The desired temperature limits—the standard—is chosen by you. The thermostat checks to see if the room temperature has decreased to its lowest allowed limit; if it has, the thermostat turns on the heater. When the temperature increases to its highest desired limit, the thermostat turns off the heater. In this way the temperature remains within a narrow range.

If one can control a thermostat, why not a group of people? As top executive, you set up requirements, goals, and measures of performance for everyone. Then you gather, or more likely get others to gather, data about competitors, department activities, employees, financial data, government activities, the market, products, research developments, stockholders, suppliers, and lots more. After massaging this data and comparing the status of the corporation in terms of the various measures of performance, you determine the extent of deviation. The next step, of course, is to introduce feedback to correct the actions of the people in the organization.

Why not, indeed? The control model became the philosophy of management in the Industrial Society. The control model is also the philosophy behind the management information system: Just supply me with all the deviations from standard and I'll make decisions to correct them.

It's about time we learned that the control model is good for machines, not for people. People are not machines. Not automotons. Not "hands" to feed the machines. Not commodities. Not order takers. In addition to hands, they come with eyes and ears and especially brains. They are smart and creative. They have their desires and aspirations. They are human.

The Mutual-Development Model

Of course, humans make mistakes. But they also learn from their mistakes. The story is told about one of Tom Watson's vice presidents at IBM making a mistake that cost the company ten million-dollars. The vice president came to Watson's office with a letter of resignation in his hand. To his surprise, here is what he was told by Watson:

> Let you go? We just spent ten million dollars giving you one hell of an education! I can't wait to see what you're going to do next.

Watson was following the *mutual-development model*, at least with respect to this vice president.The mutual-development model, like the control model, is a loop, but of an entirely different kind. In the control model people are merely pawns in the loop. In the mutual-development model, all the people involved in an effort, set standards and all of them learn.

The essence of the mutual-development model is acceptance of each person the way he is, as an autonomous individual with his own vision. The best way to influence him is to help him. There is no boss and employee, superior and inferior, teacher and student, white collar and blue collar, expert and novice. There is only an environment where everyone can develop to his peak potential.

A leader is not a boss. A leader does not push, coax or punish. A leader is concerned about each person she works with. A leader does not need to make decisions, but to be sure that the best decisions are made.

The famous philosopher Lao-tzu said:

> The bad leader is one who the people despise
>
> The good leader is he who the people praise
>
> The great leader is he who the people say:
>
> 'We did it ourselves.'

COMMUNICATE YOUR VISION

The first task of a leader is to get people excited about what she is trying to do, excited about her vision. If people get to the point where they share her vision, they will accomplish wonders.

Before you communicate with others, write your vision clearly, simply, and briefly on a single sheet of paper. Don't burden it with detail. You should be able to express your vision in one, or at most two, paragraphs.

After you have clarified your own thoughts in this way, you are ready to communicate with others. This you may do through speech, writing, and behavior. You may sprinkle it into your conversation as you would chocolate chips onto your ice cream. You may add it to your writing as you would a metaphor or a Shakespeare quotation.

A monologue, though, is not communication. It is not enough to expound your ideas. You need to get the reactions of people. You need to get them involved. You need to elicit and discuss the visions of other people in your network. All people with vision have a need to be heard, understood, and appreciated. A leader listens to these people the same way she would like them to listen to her.

Probably the best way to communicate your vision is to exemplify it. People do not follow talkers. They follow people with integrity, people who live according to their professed values.

Steve Jobs had a vision. The first time, he presented it essentially as a monologue, the second time as a dialogue.

In 1975 the vision of Steve Jobs was to bring computer power to all the people. At age 21, he dropped out of Reed College, and together with Steve Wozniak, bought a $20 computer chip, obtained other electronic parts from Atari and Hewlett-Packard, and in Jobs' garage in Los Altos, California, built the first Apple computer. The next year the two formed the Apple Computer Company and in the year after that they introduced Apple II. The desktop Apple computer was a smashing success. The company grew from nothing to Fortune 500 status in less than five years— the first company in history to accomplish such a feat!

When the company reached the billion dollar level, Jobs lured John Sculley away from Pepsi Cola to become the president of Apple Computer. Jobs remained the chairman of the board. Jobs and Sculley had different views of the future of the company. There was conflict and eventually Jobs was kicked out of the company he had founded.

What a blow! But it did not stop Jobs. He decided to found a new company. He was only thirty one. But this time he was going to do it right. This time he would be a great listener as well as a great communicator of his vision and values.

So one day in 1985 he invited several of his former colleagues at Apple to a pizza dinner at his home, where he presented his ideas for a new company. After much discussion, the group agreed to form a company called NeXt, to manufacture an advanced personal computer or workstation—the next step. The computer would have tremendous storage, voice, image and sound capabilities. It would be a new intellectual powerhouse. (Lately NeXt has shifted to software.)

The corporation itself would be an intellectual powerhouse too. People would be hired for their knowledge and an environment built to allow them to grow their knowledge. Everything would be open. There would be no secrets from anyone. Even tough negotiations with IBM and other companies would be known to every single employee in the company. There would be lots of sharing of ideas.

At NeXt, not only is there a shared vision, employees are helped to follow their own visions. Morale is high. Turnover is low.

COOPERATE WITH NETWORK MEMBERS

Volumes and volumes have been written about how to manage people so well that they will be committed to their work. Management and commitment are contradictory terms:

* Management implies *control*; commitment implies SELF-DIRECTION

* Management implies *task assignment*; *commitment implies INITIATIVE*

* Management implies *competition*; commitment implies COOPERATION.

COOPERATION—this is where it is at. To instill a shared vision, it is not enough to discuss visions. This is only talk.

Important talk, but talk. You need to cooperate with people in the pursuit of their visions. They will then find it much easier to cooperate with you in the pursuit of your vision. All of you will enjoy cooperating with each other.

Cooperation may take the form of teams within an organization and of alliances between organizations.

Teams

In recent years, as part of the quality movement, the concept of the *self-managed team* has swept over manufacturing companies. Members of these teams cooperate with each other to find solutions to quality problems. Milliken, a winner of the 1989 Malcolm Baldrige National Quality Award, has reorganized its 14,300 workers into 1700 self-management teams. Teams are spreading to non-manufacturing companies as well.

The self-managed team has become a buzzword. In many cases the team has been incorporated into the essentially hierarchical structure of the corporation. A supervisor—perhaps he has a more euphemistic title—is in charge of the self-managed team. He reports to higher-ups in a not too different manner from the way old-fashioned supervisors reported.

Merely because it is called a team does not mean that teamwork is taking place. Merely because it is called a team does not mean the members cooperate with each other. Merely because it is called a team does not mean that members have common values or visions.

But if they do, true cooperation may take place.

Cooperation boosts individualism AND teamwork.

Each person on the team contributes in her own way what she does best, always keeping in mind the good of the group. There's no conflict between this type of individualism and the common good. They are supportive of each other. All team members benefit.

To increase cooperation among employees working on different disciplines but on the same product, companies have torn down the walls separating departments. Advanced Micro Devices has set up separate directorates for each product line. Each directorate has its own engineering, manufacturing and sales people working together for a common goal.

Alliances

Cooperation is growing even among companies. Among the more famous alliances are those of General Motors and Toyota, Ford and Fiat, ATT and Olivetti, and IBM and Apple.

Altera and Cypress Semiconductor have formed an alliance. Altera designs the best program logic devices, special electronic devices which need to be fabricated into chips. It does not have facilities for chip fabrication, an entirely different specialty. Altera therefore bought a small equity position in Cypress Semiconductor, a chip fabricator. Both companies benefit: Altera has access to a chip fabrication facility it needs and gets cost savings. Cypress can run its machines closer to capacity and has rights to Altera's future products.

SETTLE ISSUES DEMOCRATICALLY

Communication and cooperation bring people together so they may be disposed towards each other's ideas and visions. But democracy is the best means for making the team cohesive. With democracy, your purpose as leader, is not to make all decisions, but to feel confident that the best decisions are made.

Everybody extolls the virtues of democracy in politics. But not in business. And yet, if you think about it, democracy in his business affairs is far more important to the average person than democracy in his political affairs. The first is very close to home. The second often is far removed.

Democracy definitely makes for better teamwork. When you know you have a voice in what happens you are more interested in affecting results. You feel like working harder because it is something you have decided is important. Because all of you in the group have had discussions and have made decisions in common, all of you feel like cooperating with each other for the common good.

RESPECT EACH PERSON'S AUTONOMY

Open communication, mutual cooperation, and effective democracy produce the type of environment for the sharing and mutual support of visions. Openness, mutuality, and effectiveness are byproducts of personal autonomy. It happens when each person trusts and treats with respect the integrity of all other persons in her network.

The quality movement in the United States has shown that respecting the autonomy of individuals brings great rewards. When those who do the work - not a quality department—are responsible for the quality of their work, they feel ownership of the work. They are treated with more respect and have more self-respect. They have that feeling of self autonomy. They produce excellent products.

At Northwestern Mutual Life Company, they used to have an army of clerks, each staring at a computer screen and doing one tiny part of the processing of applications. Boring. Interest deadening. No autonomy in any sense. The company redesigned the entire work structure to make each job more interesting. Sixty four job descriptions were converted to six. The same clerks now handle everything related to an application. They are given the tools to do it. They make phone calls, read attending physician statements, make decisions and maintain correspondence. The workers have greater self-autonomy.

In the final analysis, however, the best way to maintain self-autonomy is by keeping the company, or at least specific groups in the company, small. Even big corporations are starting to think small. Kollmorgen, which makes sophisticated electronic devices, is a high-tech conglomerate with divisions and subsidiaries around the world. Yet each division never has more than about a couple of hundred people. Each division has its own president and board of directors and is totally responsible for its own performance. Headquarters is there only for guidance, as is obvious from the fact that it consists of only seven officers and two secretaries. Robert Swiggett, head of Kollmorgen says:

> We believe that divisions which get too big lose vitality, family atmosphere and easy, informal internal communication.

LEARNING NUGGETS

To instill a shared vision within your network:

- **DON'T BE A BOSS—don't act superior and run an organization**

- **COMMUNICATE YOUR VISION**—express it clearly, communicate it often, and listen to the visions of others
- **COOPERATE WITH NETWORK MEMBERS**—work together as a team within the organization and form alliances with other organizations
- **SETTLE ISSUES DEMOCRATICALLY**—everybody should participate to make the best decisions
- **RESPECT EACH PERSON'S AUTONOMY**—self autonomy comes with respect for the individual and is best achieved in a small group.

Chapter 19

Build A Learning Community

If sharing visions is a way to build a cohesive community, sharing learning is a way to make a community strong and effective. By sharing learning I do not mean that you and other people in your network learn the same thing at the same time. Definitely not. This is impossible. Given, the same data, you and I will each learn something different. By sharing I mean that each person in the community supports others in the learning process.

A learning community is one where people help each other learn.

Whether you are building a learning community of two or twenty thousand, the community consists of people, not machines. People learn. Machines, at least today, can not learn. Neither can an organization learn, though it has become fashionable to speak of the learning organization. An organization can perform and service, produce and sell. But it can not learn. Only people in the organization are capable of learning. Only people have the brains. An organization is nothing without these brains.

The four principles for building a learning community are:

- **Avoid Organization-Mania**
- **Don't Train—Enable People to Learn**
- **Promote Discussion**
- **Run Cooperative Experiments**

AVOID ORGANIZATION-MANIA

A man becomes self-employed. Immediately he doesn't think of himself as a person, but as a business. He gathers a few colleagues together to form a larger working group. No longer does he think of these chosen few in terms of their intellectual strengths—although this is why he picked them—but as an organization. He and his working group spend a great deal of time planning the growth of the organization. They think very little of their own personal growth. The bigger the company grows the more time every member spends thinking about the organization. It seems that only the organization counts. What about the people?

Our society is infected with organization-mania.

ORGANIZATION-MANIA. The bug hit us in the Industrial Society. In the rigidly-structured pyramidal corporation, each person had his function according to the dictates of the organization. All measurements were made about the status of the organization. All information was collected and decisions made to improve the organization. The greatest good was to make the organization bigger and bigger.

More ORGANIZATION-MANIA. Computers led to automation. Only the organization counts. Why worry about people? Machines can do the tasks of people, faster and more reliably. Let the people go. Replace them with machines.

Organizations are dying from organization-mania. Organization-mania leads to organizations without people, an oxymoron.

Information for the Organization

Organization-maniacs love information. They believe that information, the more the better, gives the manager control of the organization. They are constantly pushing for bigger, grander, and more all-encompassing MISs—to help make superior decisions about the organization.

With all the information floating around, have decisions improved? Are the big corporations who have built sophisticated MISs more successful than others? No, they are not. Many have disappeared. Others have merged with other companies. Even the best of them—IBM—has fallen on hard times and has laid off thousands of employees.

We are no longer in the Industrial Society. The control model no longer applies.

Automation for the Organization

Organization-maniacs love automation.Automation, like MIS, increases executive control. How? By getting rid of people. The fewer the number of people needed to produce a product the greater the productivity or efficiency. Furthermore, you can depend upon machines. They don't stop for coffee breaks, never get sick, do not gossip, don't complain and can work around the clock. Automation is reliable.

The newest pitch of organization-maniacs is called CIM for Computer-Integrated Manufacturing. Even the best MIS does not include a raft of data associated with engineering and with production on the factory floor. The computer improved the engineering process through CAD (Computer-Aided Design) systems; and production through robots and automation systems. CIM is an integration of MIS with CAD systems and automation systems. It is a super-MIS.

A CIM system is what Allen-Bradley built in its plant in Milwaukee which produces electric motor starters for cars. It is called a stockless production system because it receives orders one day and the product is automatically manufactured, tested, packaged and shipped the next day—all without human hands. In addition to initiating the production process, the order also executes accounting, sales, and planning functions. Only a few people are needed to run the entire plant.

CIM is excellent for producing standard products. What happens when a product changes in an unexpected way? CIM produces reliability, but where is the flexibility? CIM has been balyhooed by economists, journalists, politicians, engineers, businesspeople, educators and almost everyone else as the best way to compete with the Japanese. This is nonsense. According to someone who should know, Rick Cook of *Managing Automation* magazine:

> Highly automated mass production plants of any sort
> are notoriously inflexible, and semiconductor plants
> are worse than most.

Semiconductor, or computer chip, plants are worse than most because chip technology is in a constant state of flux. Without flexibility, chip plants are almost useless. Flux is the nature of everything today. Flux is one reason for building a learning community. Flux is the reason you need to depend on people not machines.

Flexible Integration for People

Don't be an organization-maniac. An organization-maniac gets rid of people. Those that remain are turned into automotons.

Instead of building a CIM, why not build a PIN (People Integrated Network). You are not interested in control, the fetish of the hierarchical organization. You are looking for a way to build a learning community.

People make the best integrators.

PIN depends upon the same technologies as CIM: communication and computing systems. But they are used differently. Instead of reflecting the structure of the organization, in PIN the communication network is tailored to individuals. Instead of aggregating data by functional groupings which are then integrated for decision-making by managers, in PIN the information system is there to answer specific questions of individuals.

PIN has been adopted by new high-tech organizations, especially by those like Brooktree, who are pushing the state of the art in semiconductors and computers.

People integration is a concept that's right, not only for manufacturing corporations, but for all kinds of organizations: wholesale, retail, business services, personal services, education, and government.

Avoid organization-mania. If you need a mania make it people-mania.

DON'T TRAIN - ENABLE PEOPLE TO LEARN

Organization-maniacs believe in training. Through training they can take raw recruits and mold them in their, the maniacs', image. Through training, they can get novices to understand the company's technology. Through training, they can get outsiders to act like company people.

Trainers represent the organization and try to convert trainees into organization men and women. They know what is right and correct and proper; the trainees do not. The trainers show their students how to get along in the organization.

Trainers follow a top-down approach, not the ideal method to use in THE LEARNING SOCIETY. The best way to grow a learning community is not by building a training ladder, but by constructing an atmosphere conducive to people learning. This idea is expressed by prominent people in corporate "training":

CARL SYMON AT IBM—"Because we are serious about performance, we must shift our focus from instruction to *learning*."

ERNEST SAVOIE, AT FORD—"In Ford's experience, employees prefer self-directed *learning* seven to one over traditional classroom instruction."

The emphasis on learning in these statements is mine. A training program does not produce a learning community. A training program, besides being conceived by some for the enlightenment of others, usually is a one-shot deal. After you are trained, you can do the job. A learning community is one where everyone is always learning. If you, as a member, don't know something, you ask and always get a helpful reply. And if you need to be shown how to do something, the showing is part of the reply. No training. Learning. NeXt and Tandem corporations have established such a learning environment with the aid of computer work stations to encourage company-wide dialogue and discussion.

In a learning community people are always helping people learn.

PROMOTE DISCUSSION

The essence of a learning community is a Socratic environment: each person is asking questions and offering answers. If they all know only questions but no answers, they seek to discover the answers as a team.

The Socratic Attitude

To promote a Socratic environment you need a Socratic attitude. Socrates introduced the dialogue as a means of learning, both for himself and for the people he conversed with. He did not teach. He set up an environment for learning. He asked questions, received answers, and then he asked more questions. Through dialogue the two people learned together.

Dialogue works for more than two people. It is then called discussion. To have good discussions you need other people with the same Socratic attitude. People who are curious, skeptical, and eager to learn. People who do not take anything for granted. People who are always asking questions of themselves, of nature, of books, and of people around them. People who are not afraid of what the answers may be. People who take risks by trying something new in order to learn. People to whom learning and self-development is a passion.

Most of us think we are good learners when we really are not. We reach a certain level of capability and then rely on the scripts we have learned. Contrary to conventional opinion, this is more true for experts than for the rest of us. Experts want more than anything, to be right. They place new problems into old contexts to understand them. Then they proceed to apply the solutions that worked so well in the past. They follow the same old scripts.

As Robert J. Kriegel and Louis Patler say, to be a true learner you need to adopt the mindset of a beginner. Forget what you "know". Just because you have solved certain problems in the past a certain way, does not necessarily mean this is the best way today. Look at the problem in a different way. Ask questions, ask questions, ask questions. And consider each answer you get before dredging up your old scripts. More likely than not, you will end up changing your old scripts.

More than mere questions and answers are involved. Like Socrates, you must search for meaning. Interchange of information may not necessarily lead to understanding. Don't merely ask. Probe to determine if you are asking the appropriate question. Don't merely answer. Do whatever you can to assure understanding. Understanding takes time, persistence, and willingness.

Team Problem Solving

A natural outgrowth of the Socratic community is team problem solving. Each member contributes in her own way. There is a spirit of collaboration, which is easily identified when you hear members speaking of "we", not "I".

It is easy to see what is involved when two of you are working together as a team to solve a problem. After a preliminary dialogue, you subdivide the task in light of what each of you is best at. Every once in a while you get together to discuss what you are doing and to exchange opinions and ideas. You get together at the end to review what the two of you have accomplished. The two of you are a team.

The same approach may be applied to a bigger team. With more members you need a little more formality. You need a facilitator to make sure everyone does not speak at once. But not much more. The synergy achieved with a bigger group may be tremendous. I am often amazed at what is produced by brainstorming sessions of learning teams.

In a team that is a learning community, members cooperate to solve mutual problems. However, not all teams are learning communities. You hear so much these days about team planning, team organization and team management. A learning community can not be planned in the same way you may plan to introduce a product; it must be nourished Socratically. A learning community can not be organized by bringing together people with complementary aptitudes and abilities; it is their attitude toward learning, not their aptitudes and abilities that count. A learning community definitely can not be managed; it must be guided by a shared vision.

RUN COOPERATIVE EXPERIMENTS

In addition to indulging in dialogue and discussion, a learning community is constantly experimenting. How can you learn if you don't try anything new? Proclivity toward experimentation is probably the defining characteristic of the flexible network of THE LEARNING SOCIETY.

For want of better terms I call experimentation within the network, the *new engineering*; and experimentation which includes people outside the normal, more intimate, network, the *new marketing*.

The New Engineering

Within the organization of the past, there was a formidable separation of functions. There were separate departments for research and development, engineering, production, distribution, scheduling, planning. Building a product consisted of a strictly-defined step-by-step procedure which sequenced from one department to another according to a formal dance defined by management.Even if each of these multifarious groups wanted to experiment, what effect would it have on the output? Very little.

The new engineering is bringing people together to allow interdisciplinary discussions and effective experimentation. The new engineering includes all product, service, and business functions that must be done from the time the company knows what the client needs until the client is satisfied. In this new approach, what was previously performed in separate sequential steps, is accomplished in an integrated way. Some people call this approach *concurrent engineering*.

In this approach, people of different skills and specialties work together as a team to produce a product or service. In this environment discussions are countless and continuous. In this environment team members can agree on an experiment and work together to execute it. Each member learns more about her own specialty and about the common output of the team.

Many internal operations depend upon the work done by people outside the organization - suppliers, for instance. In the new engineering, suppliers are made members of the team. Some companies call these teams *partnerships*. The supplier-producer team can execute experiments to help people in both companies learn.

The New Marketing

In the old industrial company zillions of identical products were mass produced, and sold by a sales force via mass media to a mass market. Experimentation, if there was any, was associated with determining the advertisements and the sales pitches that worked best.

Today the emphasis is more on services than on products, more on intellectual services than on personal services. A service is not the same as a product. A service is not tangible. It can not be counted. A service is not rendered to a mass market. A service is something done for an individual. Discussions about a service must have a qualitative, not quantitative, tone.

With a service, most of yesterday's marketing techniques are inappropriate. We do not need sales forecasts. We do not need mass advertising. We do not need salesmen making florid presentations to customers. We do not need telemarketeers annoying prospects. Since we are not selling a product, we do not need these product-selling devices.

The new marketing consists of linking your client onto your network, making him part of your team, your learning community. You get to know your client's problems through rap sessions. You get to help him solve his problems through team effort. You get to try experiments together. You both learn in the process.

Regis McKenna, the marketing guru of Silicon Valley, describes the new marketing with the following statement:

> It is a fundamental shift in the role and purpose of marketing: from manipulation of the customer to genuine customer involvement; from telling and selling to communicating and sharing knowledge.

The following are a few examples of new marketing at work:

GENENTECH—A representative carries laptop computers with him when he visits pharmacists and physicians to sell drugs. He uses the laptop to enrich the learning dialogue by instantaneously obtaining the answer to questions about how to use specific drugs, by printing out highly technical articles presented at medical conferences, and by getting company specialists involved.

APPLE COMPUTER—In 1984, Apple launched the Macintosh computer. Several months before the launch, it offered full-day hands-on demonstration workshops to industry leaders, analysts and influential Americans. To prominent software developers, it gave the Macintosh away so they could dream up software for the new computer. To quote McKenna on this event: "Dialogue with customers and media praise were worth more than any notice advertising could buy."

XEROX—Before Xerox formally introduced its Docutech System, it placed twenty five of these systems at so-called Beta test sites. After these twenty five customers thoroughly tested them—experimented with them—they made recommendations for changes. After it made these changes, Xerox knew its new product would serve its customers well.

LEARNING NUGGETS

For a small or large network, build a learning community:

- **AVOID ORGANIZATION-MANIA—instead of seeking information and automation for the organization, try to achieve flexible integration with people**

- **DON'T TRAIN - ENABLE PEOPLE TO LEARN—learning is not the result of training. It is a self-directed activity**

- **PROMOTE DISCUSSION—a Socratic attitude in a team environment is what is needed**

- **RUN COOPERATIVE EXPERIMENTS—with the new engineering, which integrates all internal activities under one unit; and the new marketing, which adds clients to the network for mutual learning.**

Chapter 20

Manage Learning Tools For Learning Community

This is the year 2020. This is the story of Creative Craig.

The story begins in the last decade of the twentieth century. Craig was a tinkerer. Because of his constant poking around his car and other machinery, he just barely graduated high school. This depressed him. He located a job as a car mechanic. But he remained depressed, always complaining, always feeling terrible. His customers called him Crabby Craig.

One day, he felt so bad, he picked up a 22-caliber pistol and shot himself in the head. But this is not the end of the story, only the beginning. The bullet did not kill him! The bullet penetrated his brain at the exact spot which was responsible for his depression. As a result Craig was no longer depressed. He cured himself by shooting himself!

But he also lost his memory for mechanics. Suddenly he was totally unaware of how to do simple things like replacing spark plugs, changing a tire or connecting a battery. His actions were disjointed. So much so that people were beginning to call him Crazy Craig.

By this time the twenty-first century had arrived. Neurosurgeons were beginning to gain a fairly good understanding of the different functions of the different areas of the brain. A few medical researchers had discovered how to enhance sensitivity to touch, smell, and other human senses by connecting special neural networks to specific locations in the brain with super-tiny wires. A brilliant neurosurgeon connected into Craig's brain a neural implant which he hoped would assume the functions of the missing section.

The neural implant did not work. But Craig, instead of becoming depressed, was suddenly possessed by a hunch. He asked the neurosurgeon to bring a "plug" from the implant to his scalp where it would be available for external connections. The surgeon did this. The "plug" was tiny and invisible in the surrounding hair.

Now Craig began a long experimental program. He connected different types of neural devices to his brain "plug". He tried to train these devices to do certain mental tasks. He had hundreds of failures. But he did establish that his "plug" could act as a junction for connecting external devices directly to his brain. So he continued.

At this point, Craig realized that he did not have the necessary mental framework to invent the type of tool he desperately desired. So he formed a network of cognitive scientists, neurosurgeons, computer hardware and software specialists, and learning facilitators. With the aid of software learning tools tailored to the use of each of these specialists, the group continued the experiments. Two years ago the team invented a neural device which Craig was able to connect to his brain "plug". With it he was able to regain, and even improve upon, his previous motor skills!

Craig and his team were so elated that they decided to invent other neural devices and techniques for enhancing other brain functions. The team studied and experimented. It invented tiny devices other people could connect to their brains to help them enhance different brain functions. The neurosurgeon made the connections.

Today there is a jeweler in the network. Since the neural devices are so tiny, they are made ornamental. The jeweler designs earrings, bracelets, pins, pendants, rings, nose rings and hair pieces. She adds gold and gemstones to the neural devices. The team sells them as AI Gems. Here AI means

not Artificial Intelligence, but Augmented Intelligence.

I don't know if Creative Craig and his network will happen in 2020 or 2050 or if it will happen at all. Who does? But I am sure the science and technologies of the mind will unfold in dazzling and exciting ways. I am certain that flexible people networks will arise to tackle difficult intellectual tasks. I am positive that new advanced learning tools will enable members of networks to learn and help other members learn. I am confident a Creative Craig will live.

You can be almost as creative as Creative Craig today. You can form a network of independent specialists. You can exercise leadership by instilling a shared vision and converting the network into a learning community. You can manage learning tools to aid individual learners and learning helpers. The principles of learning-tool management are:

- **Don't Confuse Learning Tools with Automation**
- **Acquire Learning Tools for Individuals**
- **Develop Tools with Teamwork**
- **Build a Global Learning Landscape**

DON'T CONFUSE LEARNING TOOLS WITH AUTOMATION

Though both depend on technology, there is a tremendous difference between learning tools and automation. Automation ostensibly is for the improvement of the organization. Learning tools are for the improvement of individuals.

Automation for Organizations

Here is the Industrial-Society view. Both machines and people are boxes on a chart. If one finds that a machine can do a job "better" than a human, one replaces the human box with the machine box. If a human box needs information from a machine box, one feeds him the information. If a machine box needs information from a human box, one asks the human box to feed the information.

There's no room for visions. There's no need for learning. The human box is trained to be an automoton, like the machine box. He is shown how to feed and be fed by the machine box. No vision. No learning. Why does one need learning tools?

Learning Tools for People

Learning tools are designed for people, not organizations.

What counts is not the organization, but the individual people within it. This is why the network is the best way of viewing this organization. People have visions, which come from their "inner voices". People are eager to learn. They need learning tools to help them.

The age of mass production of physical products is gone. The need for control is gone. But the need for activities of the mind is zooming. People do not need information that is part of an organization structure, but the ability to grow their knowledge. They do not need to be trained as though they were seals, but have the opportunity to learn. They need learning tools to aid them in improving their basic skills: observation, memory, thinking, creativity, and human relations. They need tools to aid them in performance. The better they are able to learn, the more they can contribute to the organization.

As the Creative Craig story shows, the computer is becoming a personal companion. It can help the individual in all her intellectual endeavors. It can be an extension to an individual's mind. With it, the intellectual power of each person in an organization may be raised by an order of magnitude, and of the organization as a whole, by another order of magnitude.

ACQUIRE LEARNING TOOLS FOR INDIVIDUALS

A learning community is one where people help each other learn. Each person may at one time be a learner and at another time a learning helper. he learner is busy developing knowledge. The learning helper sets up conditions to help the learner. She does not train. She may be a learning facilitator like Peggy Allan, or a coach like Rou de Gravelles.

Since a person directs her own learning, her learning tools should be designed accordingly. The easiest way for a person to learn is by following the I-D-E-A loop (Inquire and Dialogue, Do and Experiment, Evaluate and Conclude, Amend and Try Again). Learning tools should help her in each step of the loop. They should help her in modeling, being creative, and communication networking.

Modeling Tools

Modeling is the forte of the computer. Software modeling tools—basic, conceptual, and dynamic—are the best way to use your companion computer. The modeling tool is a superb way to study the workings of a device or system, the proficiency of a procedure or organization, or the future results of a new technique or culture.

The basic tools model by number, word, picture, or multimedia. They may be mathematical algorithms, word processor and desk-top publishing packages, graphics illustrators and presentation systems, or authoring and instructional systems built around CD-ROM and other multi-media devices.

The conceptual tools model by data or knowledge. The data model is used for all storage and retrieval systems; and for systems based on storage and retrieval, such as inventory control, sales prospecting and computer-aided instruction. The knowledge model is at a high level of integration and introduces AI.

The dynamic tools—time management systems, simulations and computer games—enable the duplication of a series of events or possible events. They offer a way of essentially experiencing events without physically partaking of them.

Some modeling tools are very complex. Perhaps you may be able to use a tool once it is built. But you may not feel confident of trying to build it yourself. In a people network, however, there is bound to be someone who can do it.

Creativity Enhancement Tools

Creativity is needed both by learners and learning helpers. There are enhancers of intellectual creativity, such as outliners and idea processors.They help an individual organize his thoughts and find associations among different ideas or concepts. There are enhancers of artistic creativity, such as verbal, graphical, musical, and performance-arts imagination stimulators. They allow a person to try out new ideas, unusual artistic creations, different musical forms, and more effective and personalized presentations.

Communication Networking Tools

When speaking of creativity, almost everyone realizes that tools are needed for individuals, not the organization. Not so with communication networking tools. Here, the emphasis almost always is placed on the organization. But, I repeat, the greatest benefit accrues to the organization if networking tools are oriented toward the learning needs of individuals.

You are the central node in your network. You want all the tools and communication with all the information sources and people that may help you in your learning.Think of each individual you work with as being the central node of her network. She wants all the tools and communication with all the information sources and people that may help her in her learning.

DEVELOP TOOLS WITH TEAMWORK

I place a lot of emphasis on the individual. I place an equal amount of emphasis on community. Individuality and working together in a community go together like chocolate chips in a coffee cake.

In the days of the rigid pyramidal corporation it was difficult for a worker to be an individual. Each of his movements was managed by others.Today, in THE LEARNING SOCIETY, when leadership is replacing management, each person is considered to be a responsible individual. An individual has a vision. An organization has a vision, usually an extension of the founder's vision.In a community there is a sharing of visions. Individuality blooms. Responsibility blooms. Teamwork blooms.

Instead of buying an off-the-shelf standardized learning tool, a tool-building team may develop a tool according to the exact needs of the people in the organization.

The Tool-Building Team

An organization has a vision, an extension of the vision of the leader. To enlist the aid of members of the organization the leader needs to build a team. A team consisting of people with a shared vision. A team where each member can contribute as an autonomous individual. A team making decisions democratically.

Normally, a tool-building team may consist of the following:

POTENTIAL USER—A learner. Someone knowledgeable about the need for the learning tool, the nature of the user's working environment, and how the tool may be used.

DOMAIN SPECIALIST—A learning helper. Someone knowledgeable in the chosen learning area.

TOOL SPECIALIST—Someone knowledgeable about the tool-building tool, the learning tools which may be fashioned through its use, and the methods for fashioning these tools.

SOFTWARE SPECIALIST—Someone knowledge in the art of software.

The potential user is on the team to write the specifications at the beginning to make sure the appropriate learning tool is built. He knows what he needs and the working environment in which the learning tool will be used. He can also assure realistic testing of the completed tool. The domain specialist, of course, is on the team because of his understanding of the subject matter and his problem-solving know-how. The tool specialist is there for a similar reason, but with respect to the use of the tool-building tool. The software specialist is there to stretch the capabilities of the tool-building tool and to add software functions to the finished tool.

Building the Tools

The tool-building team, together with the many tool-building tools on the market, make possible the development of many learning tools. Among the tool-building tools are data base management systems, for building data base and information systems; authoring systems, for writing instructional systems; simulation tools, with which may be written simulations for the study of procedures and systems; and AI tools, for developing problem-solving advisors.

According to a commonly-held notion, AI tools can be used only by sophisticated high-priced AI-software experts. Of course there are AI tools which only such experts understand and can use. But there are plenty of AI tools which can be mastered by people not versed in AI technology.

E.I. DuPont has done this and in a big way. DuPont believes in decentralization. It is a loose confederation of business units, each concerned with a variety of technical projects. It does about $30 billion dollars of business a year with chemical, plastics and other industrial products which it manufactures in 140 different sites around the world. Employee teams, mostly small, very few with a tool specialist, have built about a thousand small AI-oriented learning tools.

One of these learning tools, the Packaging Advisor, was developed by plastic experts for the use of DuPont salesmen. When salesmen speak to bottle manufacturers, they allow the manufacturers to learn from the tool what plastic would be best for their purposes.

Team members learned enough about the AI tools from a short 2-day course. According to Ed Mahler, who is the mastermind behind all artificial intelligence activity at DuPont, 80% of problems previously solved by consultants personally are now solved by these learning tools.

BUILD A GLOBAL LEARNING LANDSCAPE

If a global learning landscape is good for you as one person, it is of superb use to your group or organization. It is vitally needed by your learning community.

Within your learning community, you may have an old-fashioned library of books and other literature. Here you no doubt want to store documents in frequent use. With the aid of a local area network (LAN), you can obtain rapid communication among network people, their computers, and their learning tools.

By connecting your group to an external network, people in your group may be able to get information they need piped in. They may also be able to cultivate their mental gardens with specialized information. They may have access to information sources and infopreneurs. They may reach global sources of information.

LEARNING NUGGETS

- **DON'T CONFUSE LEARNING TOOLS WITH AUTOMATION—automation is for organizations, learning tools are for people**

- **ACQUIRE LEARNING TOOLS FOR INDIVIDU-ALS—modeling, creativity enhancement, and networking tools for individual learners and learning helpers**

- **DEVELOP TOOLS WITH TEAMWORK—a team of user, expert, tool specialist, and software specialist is best for building important learning tools**

- **BUILD A GLOBAL LEARNING LANDSCAPE—connect your group members together and to a global learning network.**

COMMENTS

Dear Reader

I am eager to receive your comments:

About YOU:

* Your Vision
* Achieving your vision

About this book:

* Praise
* Criticism
* Suggestions
* Arguments
* Enhancements
* Other viewpoints
* Anything

Please forward your comments to:

Paul "the soarING" Siegel
c/o *Learning Society Publications*
3461 Marna Avenue
Long Beach, CA 90808

SUMMARY

VISION

Don't plan for an uncertain job future. Design it as you desire it around a personal vision—your dream, which acts as a star to guide you, and a magnet to keep you on course.

LEARNING

To achieve your vision you need to spend a lifetime learning about you, your areas of interest, and your environment. More so today than ever before. Because we are in THE LEARNING SOCIETY, with its emphasis on the world of ideas, not products.

LEARNING TOOLS

The computer is your major device for learning. It's a vessel that can hold an infinite variety of tools—software—for: learning an infinite variety of subjects; building learning tools to help associates learn; and communicate with and learn from colleagues and experts around the Globe.

LEADERSHIP

Today, you must think like an entrepreneur, regardless of what your vision is. This is the age of the individual, since only individuals can learn, not organizations. Instead of thinking of yourself as part of an organization, consider yourself to be the central node of a flexible network of people. You must exercise leadership.

VISION

To Guide Your Future

ENVISION YOUR "OWN THING"

* Don't Follow Others
* Don't Rely On Experts
* Don't Rely On Tests
* Listen to Your "Inner Voice"

FORGET MENTAL CONSTRAINTS

* Disregard Weaknesses
* Count on Your Strengths
* Depend on Your Drive
* Consider Sources of Help

AFFIRM YOUR VALUES

* Foster Cooperation
* Give Intellectual and Emotional Support
* Build Participatory Democracy
* Be a Global Citizen

MAKE IT A MOVIE—NOT SNAPSHOTS

* Don't Focus on Goals
* Write a Full-length-life Movie
* Run Your Own Drama
* Critique Your Unfinished Symphony

LEARNING

To Achieve Your Vision

SEEK KNOWLEDGE—NOT INFORMATION

* Don't Be an Information Sponge
* **I**—Inquire and Dialogue
* **D**—Do and Experiment
* **E**—Evaluate and Conclude
* **A**—Amend and Try Again

TAKE RISKS FOR CREATIVITY

* Break Your Habits of Thought
* Stretch Your Imagination
* Evaluate Your Intuitions
* Embroider Your Rationality

DIRECT YOUR OWN LEARNING

* Don't Submit to Educators
* Design Your Own Learning Program
* Choose Your Own Learning Collaborators
* Choose Your Own Learning Experiences

MAKE LEARNING A LIFETIME HABIT

* Be an Observer
* Cultivate Your Creativity
* Balance Analysis with Intuition
* Be a Person of Action
* Excel in Human Relations

LEARNING TOOLS

To Enhance Your Learning

DESIGN YOUR GLOBAL LEARNING LANDSCAPE

* Design Your Learning Headquarters
* Acquire Tool-building Tools
* Maintain Your Learning Headquarters

NOURISH YOUR GARDEN OF KNOWLEDGE

* Illuminate it with Your Library
* Pipe in New Information
* Cultivate it with Specialized Information

ENJOY THE FRUITS OF YOUR GARDEN

* Learn New Domains
* Enhance Mental Performance
* Acquire a Skill
* Study a System
* Stretch Your Imagination

APPLY WISDOM OF OTHER GARDENS

* Communicate with Colleagues
* Network with Community Members
* Consult with Infopreneurs

LEADERSHIP

To Enlist Others in Your Vision and Learning

INSTILL A SHARED VISION
* Communicate Your Vision
* Cooperate with Network Members
* Settle Issues Democratically
* Respect Each Person's Autonomy

BUILD A LEARNING COMMUNITY
* Avoid Organization-mania
* Don't Train—Enable People to Learn
* Promote Discussion
* Run Cooperative Experiments

MANAGE LEARNING TOOLS FOR LEARNING COMMUNITY
* Don't Confuse Learning Tools with Automation
* Acquire Learning Tools for Individuals
* Develop Tools with Teamwork
* Build a Global Learning Landscape

NOTES AND REFERENCES

Chapter 1

DEFINING SUCCESS Christopher Morley is quoted in *Working Smart*, by Michael Le Boeuf, McGraw Hill, 1979. Napoleon Hill writes in Semester 2 of *University of Success*, edited by Og Mandino, Bantam Books, 1982. The book is a treasure trove of good philosophy for living.

Chapter 2

MAKING IT HAPPEN See Robert B. Tucker's article "Dr. Waitley on How to Enhance Performance," *The Toastmaster*, June 1, 1983, page 24.

ALBERT EINSTEIN See Aylesa Forsee's *Albert Einstein—Theoretical Physicist,* Macmillan, 1963

WAYNE BARTON Michael Ryan in "Why Kids Love This Cop," *Parade*, August 5, 1990.

Chapter 3

ROLE MODELS See these biographies: William L. Shirer, *Ghandi—A Memoir,* Simon & Schuster, 1979; Frank Donovan, *The Thomas Jefferson Papers*, Dodd Mead & Co, 1963; Rheta Childe Dorr, *Susan B. Anthony,* AMS Press, 1928 (reprinted 1970); Roy L. Hill, *Rhetoric of Racial Revolt* (about King), Golden Bell Press, Denver, CO, 1964.

INDIVIDUALITY Wayne W. Dyer, *You'll See It When You Believe It*, William Morrow, 1989.

ALBERT EINSTEIN See Aylesa Forsee's *Albert Einstein—Theoretical Physicist,* Macmillan, 1963

TESTS ARE UNRELIABLE Andrew J. Strenio Jr's book, *The Testing Trap*, Rawson, Wade Publ, 1981, tells about the farcical Stanford-Binet machinations and the Koko story.

CHANGING TEST RESULTS Arthur Wimbey, "You Can Learn to Raise Your IQ Score," *Psychology Today*, 1976.

WORDSWORTH From Calm is the Fragrant Air.

Chapter 4

"FAILURE MESSAGES" A.L. Williams, *All You Can Do Is All You Can Do*, Oliver-Nelson, 1988.

MEMORY   Mort Herold, *You Can Have a Near Perfect Memory*, Contemporary Books, 1982.

THINKING   See Beverly-Colleene Galyean's article "Expanding Human Intelligence," *The Futurist*, October 1983, p. 66.

CREATIVITY   Roger Schank, *The Creative Attitude*, Macmillan, 1988, p.6.

YOU CAN DO MORE THAN YOU THINK   Schulz is quoted in Edwin C. Bliss' *Doing It Now*, Charles Scribner & Son, 1983.

BE AWARE OF YOUR STRENGTHS   Joe Batten, *Tough Minded Leadership*, Amacom, 1989.

ALBERT EINSTEIN   See Aylesa Forsee's *Albert Einstein—Theoretical Physicist*, Macmillan, 1963

STUDY ON PERSONAL DRIVE   David G. Savage, "Key to Success is Drive, Not Talent," *L.A. Times*, Feb. 17, 1985.

ABRAHAM LINCOLN'S FAILURES   See A. L. Williams, *All You Can Do Is All You Can Do*, Oliver-Nelson, 1988.

HANDICAPPED PERSON WITH DRIVE   Clay Evans presents the story about Mark Wellman's climb in "Paraplegic Gets to Top in 80 Day Yosemite Climb," *L.A. Times*, July 27, 1989.

THE CATALYST   Carl R. Rogers, *Freedom to Learn*, Charles E. Merrill, 1969.

Chapter 5

YOU NEED PEOPLE   The Manville story is given by Paul Brodeur in *Outrageous Misconduct: The Asbestos Industry on Trial*, Pantheon Books, 1985. And the Johnson and Johnson story by "Hard Decision to Swallow," *TIME*, March 3, 1986, p. 59.

EXAMPLES OF DEMOCRACTIC COMPANIES   See Robert Levering's book, *100 Best Companies to Work for in America*, Addison-Wesley Publ, 1984, and Matt Rothman's article, "A Peek Inside the Black Box," *California Business*, April 1990.

GLOBAL CITIZENSHIP   Octavio Paz's Noble lecture, "In Search of the Present," is in *The New Republic* of January 7, 1991.

COMPETITION IS BAD   A very good case is made against competition by Alfie Kohn, in *No Contest: The Case Against Competition*, Houghton Mifflin, 1986.

COOPERATION IS GOOD   See Ashley Montagu, *Growing Young*, McGraw Hill, 1981, p. 109.

Chapter 6

ALL THE WORLD'S A STAGE   From Shakespeare's *As You Like It*, Act II, Sc 7, line 139.

JIMMY CARTER   One article that describes his doings pretty well is "Carter Redux," *N.Y. Times Magazine*, Dec 10, 1989, p. 38, col 1.

THE THREE BOXES OF LIFE Richard N. Bolles, *The Three Boxes of Life*, Ten Speed Press, Berkeley, 1978.

ENJOYING WORK Kenyon Cox, *Work*, 1895.

THE UNEXAMINED LIFE Socrates, *Apology*, 38.

Chapter 7

SOCRATES Cora Mason, *Socrates—The Man Who Dared to Ask,* The Beacon Press, 1953.

ECONOMIC STATISTICS A good economic view is given by Robert Hamrin in *America's New Economy,* Franklin Watts, 1988.

JONATHAN LIVINGSTON SEAGULL See Richard Bach's classic, *Jonathan Livingston Seagull*, Macmillan, 1970.

Chapter 8

LEARNING AND SCHOOLING See the transforming book by Marilyn Ferguson, *The Aquarian Conspiracy,* St. Martin's Press, 1980, p. 288.

QUESTIONING Arno Penzias, *Ideas and Information*, W.W. Norton & Co., 1989.

LISTENING FOR UNDERSTANDING See classical article by Carl R. Rogers & F.J. Roethlisberger, "Barriers and Gateways to Communication," *Harvard Business Review*, November 1991, pp 105-111.

ROGER BANNISTER The story of how Bannister planned his triumph is described by George Sullivan in *Sports—Great Lives,* Charles Scribner's, 1988.

Chapter 9

MENTAL BLOCKS Roger von Oech follows an innovative approach to present his ideas about creativity in *A Whack on the Side of the Head,* Warner Communications, 1983.

CREATIVE THINKING Roger Schank shows that creativity is an attitude in *The Creative Attitude,* Macmillan, 1988. Another good book on creativity is Gerard I. Nierenberg's *The Art of Creative Thinking*, Simon & Schuster, 1982. Also Edward DeBono's *New Think*, Basic Books, 1968

FEAR OF MISTAKES Elbert Hubbard's quote is in *Psycho Cybernetics,* Maxwell Maltz, Prentice-Hall, 1960. John Keats's quot is in Chapter 5 of Og Mandino's *University of Success*, Bantam Books, 1982.

CREATIVITY AND KNOWLEDGE Sidney J. Parnes, "Learning Creative Behavior," *The Futurist*, August 1984, p. 30-32.

PROBLEM SOLVING AI researcher Herbert Simon states this on page 28 of *The Cerebral Symphony*, William H. Calvin, Bantam Books, 1990. It's worthwhile reading the entire book.

FOUR PHASES OF CREATIVITY Thomas R. Blakeslee, *The Right Brain*, Anchor Press, 1980.

ALBERT EINSTEIN See Aylesa Forsee's *Albert Einstein—Theoretical Physicist*, Macmillan, 1963

PAINTING IS A SCIENCE The quotation by the painter John Constable appears in Howard Gardner's *Frames of Mind*, Basic Books, 1985.

MUSICAL INTELLIGENCE The quotation by the composer Tchaikovsky appears in K.J. Gilhooly's *Thinking—Directed, Undirected, Creative*, Academic Press, 1982.

Chapter 10

EDUCATION AND HUMAN LIBERTY See John Holt, *Instead of Education*, E.P. Dutton, 1976, p. 8.

TEACHERS AS LEARNING FACILITATORS Carl R. Rogers, *Freedom to Learn*, Charles E. Merrill, 1969, p. 103.

TEACHER PEGGY ALLAN See "Peggy Allan: Let Your Students Lead You," *Learning'89*, Sept. 1989.

COACH ROU DE GRAVELLES Know from personal experience. You can reach him at 225 Carnation Ave, Corona del Mar, CA 92625.

TV TRUTH VERSUS "FACTS" See Arthur J. Cordell's article "Preparing for the Challenges of the New Media," in the *Futurist*, March 1991, p. 22.

Chapter 11

HABITS Dryden's quote appears in Semester 4 of *University of Success*, by Og Mandino, Bantam Books, 1982.

INTUITION Jonas Salk's quote is in Philip Goldberg's *The Intuitive Edge*, Jeremy B. Tarcher, 1983.

MASTERING YOUR MEMORY From William James, *Princiiples of Psychology*, Dover Publications, 1890, p. 662.

Chapter 12

KURT GOLDSTEIN STORY Jonathan Miller, editor, *States of Mind*, Pantheon Books, 1983.

INTELLIGENCE A great scientific book for the layperson, is Howard Gardner's *Frames of Mind*, Basic Books, 1983. See also, Roger Shank, The Creative Attitude, Macmillan, 1988.

Chapter 13

COMPUTERS IN THE HOME Marvin Cetron & Owen Davies, *American Renaissance: Our Life at the Turn of the 21st Century*, St. Martin's Press, 1989.

LOTUS 1-2-3

FUTURE DEVELOPMENTS Here are but a few articles: Albert Gore, "Information Superhighways," *The Futurist*, Jan/Feb 1991; Mark Fritz, "EyePhones, DataSuits and Cyberspace," *CBT Directions*, June 1990; and Tracy L. Nathan, "Computer Visualization," *The Futurist*, May 1990.

Chapter 14

ON-LINE INFORMATION   See John H. Everett, *Information for Sale*, TAB Books, 1988; also David Chandler's *Dialing for Data*, Random House, 1984.

SEARCHING DATA BASES   See David Chandler's *Dialing for Data*, Random House, 1984

dBASE   Produced by Borland, 100 Borland Way, Scott Valley, CA 95066

DIALOG   Located at 3460 Hillview Avenue, Palo Alto, CA 94304.

DOW JONES/NEWS RETRIEVAL   P.O. Box 300, Princeton, NJ 08540

MEAD DATA CENTRAL   9393 Springboro Pike, P.O. Box 933, Dayton, OH 45401.

ORBIT   Write SDC, 2500 Colorado Avenue, Santa Monica, CA 90406

BRS   1200 Route 7, Latham, NY 12110

LEXIS   Supplied by Mead Data Central (See above)

NEXIS   Supplied by Mead Data Central (See above)

MEDLINE   Supplied by National Library of Medicine, MEDLARS Management Section, 8600 Rockville Pike, Bethesda, MD 20209

Chapter 15

MAMMALS: A MULTIMEDIA ENCYCLOPEDIA   Produced by National Geographic Society. See Mark Fritz, "Multimedia and the Holy Grail," *CBT Directions*, Jan 1991.

WHERE IN THE WORLD IS CARMEN SANDIEGO   Victor F. Zonana, "PC's, Education Softwasre Move to the Head of Class," *L.A. Times,* Dec 27, 1987.

LOGO   A commercial product, LogoWriter, is available from Logo Computer Systems, 3300 Cote Vertu, Suite 201, Montreal, PQ h4R 2B7

THE MAGIC FLUTE   Produced by Warner New Media. See "Mozart's Magic," *CBT Directions,* Aug 1990.

TAXCUT   TaxCut is produced by MECA Software, 55 Walls Dr, Fairfield, Ct 06430.

SAM   Developed by Dr. Susan Athey, Assistant Professor, Computer Information Systems Dept, College of Business, Colorado State University.

FLYING SIMULATOR   The Flight Simulator is produced by Microsoft Corp, 1 Microsoft Way, Redmond, WA 98052.

TREE-CUTTING SIMULALTOR   Mark Lembersky's logger learning device is described by Mark Fritz in "Computers that Work with Wood,"*CBT Directions,* Oct 1989.

MARKET SHARE   Designed as part of a 5-day marketing management course at Nynex Corp. See Alan Richter, "Board Games for Managers," *Training & Development Journal*, July 1990.

SIMCITY   Sold by Maxis Software. See Rawley Cooper, "From Fun and Games to Effective Learning" (about SimCity), *CBT Directions,* October 1990.

MAXTHINK   Produced by MaxThink, Inc., 230 Crocker Ave, Piedmont, CA 94610. See William Hershey, "MaxThink," *BYTE*, July 1985, p. 279-284.

AUTOCAD   Produced by Autodisk Co, 2320 Marinship Way, Sausalito, CA 94965.

COREL DRAW   Produced by Corel Systems Corp, 1600 Carling Avenue, Ottawa, ON K1A 8R7.

COMPUTER ART   Melvin L. Prueitt, *Art and the Compputer*, McGraw Hill, 1984, p. 2. Also see Saul Bernstein & Leo McGarry, *Making Art on Your Computer,* Watson-Guptill Publ, 1986.

Chapter 16

COMPUSERVE   See David Chandler's *Dialing for Data*, Random House, 1984.

NETWORKING   Howard Rheingold, "I Want to Turn You On," *PUBLISH,* Feb 1992, p. 40.

INFOPRENEURS   Dan Cody, "Here Come the 'Infopreneurs'", *Sky*, November 1990.

Chapter 17

ORGANIZATIONAL NETWORKS   Jessica Lipnack & Jeffrey Stamps, *The Networking Book*, Rutledge & Kagan, 1986.

COMPANIES WILL BE SMALL   See the book by Marvin Cetron & Owen Davies, *American Renaissance*, 1984; and the articles "Coming of Age" and "Doubting Thomas" (Tom Peters thoughts), both in *INC*, 1989.

DEMOCRATIC LEADERS   Joe Batten, *Tough Minded Leadership*, Amacom, 1989.

EXAMPLES OF DEMOCRATIC LEADERS   Electro Scientific and Donnelly Mirrors are described in Robert Levering's book, *100 Best Companies to Work for in America*, Addison-Wesley Publ, 1984. A good article on NeXt is Matt Rothman's "A Peek Inside the Black Box," *California Business*, April 1990.

TRANSFORMATION OF RALPH STAYER   Ralph Stayer describes his personal transformation in "How I Learned to Let My Workers Lead," *Harvard Business Review,* November 1990.

Chapter 18

MUTUAL DEVELOPMENT MODEL   The Watson quote appears in Robert J. Kriegel and Louis Patler, *If It Ain't Broke - Break It,* Warner Books, 1991, p. 34. Also see Ricardo Semler, *Maverick*, Warner Books, 1993; Allan R. Cohen & David L. Bradford, *Influence Without Authority,* John Wiley & Sons, 1990; and Peter M. Senge, *The Fifth Discipline* (the Lao-tzu quote), Chapter 18.

COMMUNICATE YOUR VISION   Matt Rothman, "A Peek Inside the Black Box," *California Business,* April 1990.

ALLIANCES   John Case, "Intimate Relations," *Inc,* Aug 1990, p. 64-70.

SELF-AUTONOMY AND SMALL GROUP   See both of Robert Lever-ing's books: *100 Best Companies to Work for in America,* Addison-Wesley Publ, 1984; and *A Great Place to Work,* Random House, 1988. The statistics are given in "The Joy of Working," *Inc,* Nov 1987, p. 61-66.

Chapter 19

ALLEN-BRADLEY AUTOMATION   Albert Madwed, "Factories of the Fu-ture," in *The Future: Opportunity, Not Destiny,* World Future Society, 1989, chapter 3.

CIM IS INFLEXIBLE   Rick Cook, "Chipmaking: Will Bigger Plants Still be Better," *Managing Automation,* July 1989, p. 74.

ENABLE PEOPLE TO LEARN   The quotations come from Patricia A. Galagan, "IBM Faces the Future," T*raining & Development Journal,* March 1990, p. 34; and Ernest Savoie, "Ford Commits to High-Tech Training," *CBT Directions,* Dec 1988, p. 4.

THINK LIKE A BEGINNER   Robert J. Kriegel & Louis Patler, *If It Ain't Broke—Break It,* Warner Books, 1991.

THE NEW MARKETING   Regis McKenna, "Marketing is Everything," *Harvard Business Review,* Jan/Feb 1991, p. 65.

Chapter 20

CREATIVE CRAIG   This is based on a true story. See Thomas H. Maugh II, ".22-Caliber Surgery," *L.A. Times.*

AI AND DUPONT   An interesting discussion of Dupont, as well as several other companies active in artificial intelligence, occurs in Edward Feigen-baum's *Rise of the Expert Company*, Times Books, 1988.

INDEX

ORDERING INFORMATION

(Not an order form - so you can maintain this book in good condition)

To obtain a copy of this book:

1. Make out a check or money order for:

		California Residents
		California Residents

Price:	$17.95	$17.95
		8.25% Sales Tax <u>1.48</u>
		19.43
Shipping:	<u>2.50</u>	<u>2.50</u>
	$20.45	$21.93

2. Send it with a request for **DESIGN YOUR FUTURE** to:

   Learning Society Publications
   3461 Marna Ave, Suite 102
   Long Beach, CA 90808

3. Include Your:

   Name
   Affiliation
   Address
   City - State - Zip

The book will be shipped via U.S. Postal Service at the *book rate*. Please allow 3 to 4 weeks for receipt of book.
Thank you.

All books are sold with **unconditional money-back guarantee.** Ship the book back so that it reaches us in saleable condition, and your money will be refunded.